August 29, 1986

The
Annual
Of
American
Architecture
1982

THE AMERICAN INSTITUTE OF ARCHITECTS

ISBN 0-913962-30-9

The following firms, through their advertising support of the Mid-May 1982 issue of the AIA JOURNAL, have helped make possible this review of American architecture:

Allied Corp.; Alma Desk Co.; Alply Division, Subsidiary of Stolle Corp.; Alumiline Corp.; Amarlite/Anaconda; American Enka; American Gas Association; American Standard, USPP; Andersen Corp.; Architectural Engineering Products; Arco Chemical Co.; Armstrong; Atlas Door Corp.; Benjamin Moore & Co.; Brick Institute of America; Buchtal U.S.A.; Buckingham-Virginia Slate Corp., Samuel Cabot, Inc.; Cambium, Division of L. Vaughn Co.; Cheney Flashing Co.; CNA Insurance; Cold Spring Granite Co.; Columbia Lighting, Inc.; Concrete Reinforcing Steel Institute; Consolidated Aluminum Corp.; Construction Specialties, Inc.; Cookson Rolling Doors; Copper Development Association, Inc.

Databasics; Delta Faucet; Donn Corp.; Dover Corp.; Dryvit Systems, Inc.; DuPont Co., Antron, Corian, and Roofing Membrane Divisions; Duratherm Window Corp.; Ebco Manufacturing, Inc.; Efco; Elk Roofing; Elkay Manufacturing Co.; Endura;

Envirospec, Inc.; Epic Metals Corp.; Follansbee Steel Corp.; Ford Glass Division; General Electric Silicone; Georgia Marble Co.; G. F. Business Equipment, Inc.; Gold Bond Building Products Division, National Gypsum Co.

Hamilton Adams; The E. F. Hauserman Co.; Halsey Taylor, Division of King-Seeley Thermos Co.; Haws Drinking Faucet Co.; Helios Industries, Inc.; Homasote Co.; Honeywell, Inc.; Howe Furniture; Howmet Aluminum Corp., Architectural Products Division; Hunter Douglas; Integrated Ceilings, Inc.; International Masonry Institute; Inryco, Inc.; Jewett Refrigerator Co.; Kalwall Corp.; Kawneer Architectural Products; Knoll International; Koh-I-Noor Rapidograph, Inc.; Kohler Co.; Kroin.

Lees Carpets, Division of Burlington; Levolor Lorentzen, Inc.; Libbey-Owens-Ford Co.; Library Bureau; Lighting Associates, Inc.; Ludowici-Celadon; Manville Products Corp., Building Systems Division; Marvin Windows; W. B. McGuire Co., Inc.; McPhilben Lighting; Medusa Cement Co.; Meisel Photochrome Corp.; Modernfold; Monsanto Co.; R. C. Musson Rubber Co.; Nucor Corp., Vulcraft Division; Olympic

Stain; Oravisual Co., Inc.; Owens-Corning Fiberglas Corp.; Peerless Electric Co.; PSAE, CFMS and Masterspec; PPG Industries, Glass Division; Rambusch; Rixson-Firemark, Inc.; Roberts-Gordon; H. H. Robertson; Rock of Ages.

Sandell Manufacturing Co.; Schindler Haughton Elevator Corp.; Schlage Lock Co.; Sculpture Placement; Joseph E. Seagram & Sons; Shand, Morahan & Co., Inc.; Sherle Wagner International, Inc.; Sloan Valve Co.; Society of Plastics Industries, Inc.; Stanley Works, the Hardware Division/Construction; Stark Ceramics, Inc.; Steelcraft/American Standard; Sun-Dor-Co., Inc.; Summitville Tiles, Inc.; Tamko; Thiokol Specialty, Chemical Division; Tubelite; Tyler Elevator Co.; Unistrut—GTE Sylvania; USS Chemical; U.S. Gypsum Co.; U.S. Steel Corp.; Vecta Contract; Ventarama Skylight Corp.; Von Duprin, Inc.; Wayne-Dalton Corp.; Welsbach Lighting; Wilsonart: Won-Door; Wool Bureau, Inc.

Published by
The American Institute of Architects
1735 New York Avenue, N.W.
Washington, D.C. 20006

Foreword

Each year the AIA JOURNAL, monthly magazine of the American Institute of Architects, puts together a collection of notable new buildings that best signify the current trends and movements in American architectural design—the "state of the art" of architecture in this country at this time.

The term "best" has to be subjective, of course, given limitations of time and human judgment. In the case of the JOURNAL's annual review of new work, the judgments are those of the editors and of distinguished architects who sit on AIA design juries.

The first set of buildings are the editors' choice of work completed since Jan. 1, 1981. Some have been published individually in other magazines, but they appear together for the first time in this annual review, so that they can be viewed in adjacency rather than in isolation.

Next comes a set of essays on current directions in American architecture, a fixture of this annual since its inception. In past years, however, we have sought the views of architects and architectural critics and historians. This year we have sought "outside" views from a varied group of prominent Americans in other fields.

Finally come the winners of AIA's annual honor awards, America's highest honor for individual works of architecture, and a selection of awards bestowed by AIA's state and local organizations.

This volume contains the core of the JOURNAL's 1982 annual review, minus the advertising content of the issue in which it originally appeared. Advertisers in that issue are across page.

Contents

The following members of the AIA JOURNAL staff were
responsible for creation of the contents of this volume:
Donald Canty, Editor in Chief; Carole Palmer, Art Direc-
tor; Suzy Thomas and Anne Fitzpatrick, Associate Art
Directors; Stanley Abercrombie, AIA, Andrea Oppen-
heimer Dean, Mary E. Osman, Senior Editors; Allen Free-
man, Managing Editor; Nora Richter Greer, Associate
Editor; Lynn Nesmith, Editorial Assistant; Jesse Sims,
Production Manager. Publisher of the JOURNAL is Michael
J. Hanley, and general manager is David S. Godfrey.

Shining Vessel of Religious Thought

Richard Meier's Hartford, Conn., Seminary.
By Donald Canty

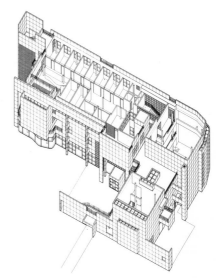

All right, this is another gleaming, ship-like, enameled Richard Meier composition, a variation on a theme he has been plying for several years. But what's wrong with staying with and perfecting a consistent theme? Does every commission require invention of a new esthetic?

Also, this may be the most exhilerating variation yet: a highly rhythmic, even syncopated composition of forms and surfaces, light and shadow. And more is demanded of it than such other recent variations as the Atheneum in New Harmony, Ind. (see the 1980 edition of the annual review).

The Hartford Seminary was founded in 1834 by the Pastoral Union of Connecticut for the traditional purpose of preparing the young for the ministry in suitably traditional surroundings, first in East Windsor and more recently in Hartford itself. The seminary today serves other and more complicated purposes. It is partly a continuing education institution for clergy and lay people in midcareer, partly a research facility, partly a resource and conference center for community as well as religious groups. There is a full-time faculty of 14 and a support staff of 12.

The seminary is not lavishly endowed, and Meier had to serve these multiple purposes within a definitely finite budget. He responded by reducing the program to an essential duality and organizing the building around it. He expresses the duality as being between "partly cloistered, inward-looking spaces" and a reaching out to the world. In other words, he put the major public spaces on the ground floor perimeter and the offices and seminar rooms upstairs.

He did something else as well: He achieved high spatial drama unusual to his work (or anyone's) in the rooms most expressive of the seminary's fundamental functions.

Vertical volumes join the building's intricately interlocking spaces (see axonometric), often with views from one to the other. Front elevation (above and preceding pages) is the most complex.

9

Far right, the altar projects out from beneath the chapel's hooded roof. Right below, curving wall wraps around the adjacent meeting room. Below, the entry court viewed from the side.

Steve Rosenthal

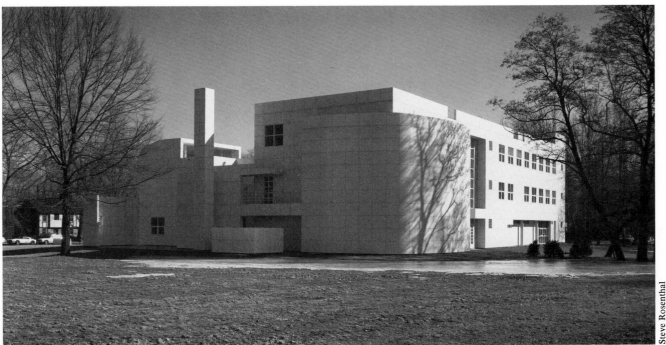

Steve Rosenthal

An enveloping welcome and changing faces.

For all of its functional and spatial achievements, what first catches one's breath about the seminary is, of course, its form. This is a remarkable sculptural object (with remarkable presence for a building of 27,000 square feet), and it changes constantly with the vantage point. No two elevations are alike.

Walls pop out to receive light through interstitial glass, the roof of the chapel arcs gently, a curving wall wraps around the meeting room that is the other major public space. The variations outside bespeak variations of use and space inside.

Once in a while, of course, there is a gesture for its own sake. And at the entry there is a kind of ceremony of planes. A screen wall passes across the face of the building at this point, penetrated by an opening on axis with the entry door, creating a transitional courtyard (entered also from a path from the parking lot to the side). The entry door itself is projected outward in a small foyer. The building thus envelops you gradually as you walk in, then once in provides a generous welcoming gesture of volume and light (next page).

The seminary sits near the center of a four-acre greensward that nicely shows off its sculptural qualities and buffers it from the neighbors. These include, on one side, the seminary's former neo-Gothic campus (now the University of Connecticut's law school), and on two other rows of workaday New England houses, most of three stories, of the kind that gladdens hearts of asbestos shingle salesmen. There was little for Meier to relate to except for some neocolonial houses on the fourth side. Meier claims a relationship of the seminary to colonial New England, but one of feel rather than form: of crispness and whiteness. The fenestration, three-foot-square panes of glass used in various kinds of clusters, also contributes to this feel.

11

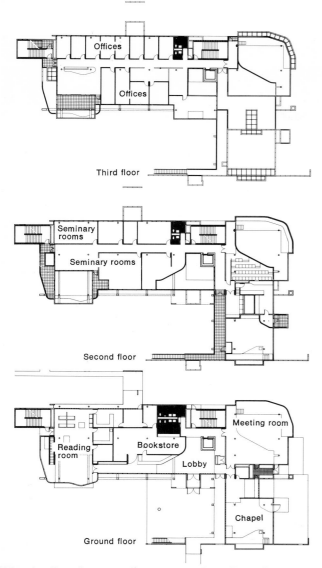

Third floor

Second floor

Ground floor

Vertical volumes that organize the plan.

Major volumes occur at the lobby and in the chapel and meeting room, the latter two aligned along the north side. These are soaring, emphatically vertical spaces. The chapel is a celebration of light, which enters through clerestories and bathes the altar almost theatrically. The light is such that the high, white ceiling all but curves out of sight, giving a sense of infinity to the volume. Meier designed an almost Wrightian bench and lectern for the chapel. (A less fortunate detail is an industrial pipe communion rail, removable and happily removed in the picture at left.)

An unusual element of the chapel is the presence of four tiny balconies at the second level corners, each with its own entry door and each capable of accommodating no more than two or three people. They serve, says Meier, for people who want to drop in and out of services unobtrusively. They are also useful for all manner of musical, liturgical and oratorical special effects.

The chapel is the seminary's most spiritual space, in character as well as use, and also, on the outside, the most dramatic punctuation point of the form, making an L of what would have been a rectangle. Yet it was not in the program. The slightly strapped seminary was all for flexibility and multiple uses. Its thought was that a classroom could double as chapel. Meier had to convince his clients that the combination was incompatible, and that a seminary without a chapel seemed an anomaly—"little more than an office building." Fortunately, he was persuasive.

The adjacent meeting room was always a key part of the program. It is very multiple in its uses—at various times a lecture hall, a concert hall, even a theater. There is access and seating at all three levels of the building.

This is a moving, almost swirling volume. Its plan closely echoes the arc of the chapel roof.

Across page, the soaring, luminous chapel, which protrudes to flank the entry court and give the plan its L shape. Top, the lobby looking toward the reading room. The bookstore is behind the reception desk. Above, the meeting room.

13

Top, the pleasingly sinuous space of the reading room. Above, a seminar room, whose pleasant but plainspoken treatment is typical of the building's working spaces. Also typical of these spaces is the fenestration, clustering four of the modular lights.

'Light is the dominating presence.'

Among other key program elements were a library and bookstore. These have not fared so well. The bookstore is in an entirely enclosed internal space on the first floor. It is not a very pleasant place to be, perhaps seeming all the more dim and cramped because of the volume and light elsewhere. The library stacks are even more unhappily embowled, being in an absolutely undisguised basement. All in all, in a place of learning, it is a strange and shabby way to treat books.

In Meier's defense, the open stacks originally were intended to be closed. Now there is not even a librarian at the seminary. But the library is considerably redeemed by the first floor reading room, perhaps the building's most completely comfortable space. Volume, multiple light sources, curving walls, fenestration, appointments, all combine here in an architectural experience of a high order.

Meier had a knowledgeable client in Dr. John Dillenberger, president of the seminary, and left him an enthusiastic one. Says a descriptive flyer handed to seminary visitors: "The different spaces [of the building] flow into each other while maintaining their own character. White and seemingly austere, the spaces highlight passage of color and, most importantly, the human ambiance of intimacy and openness. Light is the dominating presence, a single source serving multiple purposes, with new vistas meeting one at many turns."

Amen. ☐

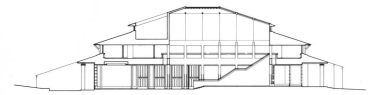

Arcadian House of the Intellect

Two views of Kallmann, McKinnell & Woods' headquarters of the American Academy of Arts and Sciences in Cambridge.

Robert Campbell: This is a series of personal footnotes to a building.

I can't do anything objective on the American Academy of Arts and Sciences because of my own involvement with it.

I should detail what that involvement was. Lawrence Anderson, former dean of architecture and planning at MIT, a member of the academy and its architectural adviser for the proposed new headquarters building, asked me to join a committee of four to choose an architect. After we had selected Kallmann, McKinnell & Wood, I continued as a part-time consultant to the academy to co-ordinate the process of design and construction.

From the beginning it seemed that all the stars were properly aligned for this new building. The academy was an architect's dream project. The Cambridge, Mass., site was a prize: five and one-half acres of wooded knoll within 10 minutes' walk of Harvard Square. The client had ample money, sensitivity and ambition. More than once, during the search for an architect and afterward, officers of the academy said they hoped for a "great" building or "a building that would be in the architectural history books."

Even the brief was almost a Beaux-Arts idealization, calling for a range of small and large spaces to be domestic in scale yet to possess a ceremonial character rare in our time.

The programmer was Dean Anderson. His program was and is a model of the art. It is short (12 pages) yet goes far beyond merely defining areas and functions into the trickier task of defining architectural character. Here are some excerpts:

"It is not necessary to assert a strongly visible presence in the community. Indeed a facade that 'claims' too much would be an affront to the conservative, well-kept houses nearby. . . . It would be as well not to be able to see the entire building at once. . . .

"Internally the general impression need not perhaps be so low-keyed as the external one, but the individual should feel at ease rather than in awe. Fruitful conversation is the academy's stock in trade, and the word implies small groups even if multitudes are present. . . .

"The academy does not want to become the vehicle for a personal or trendy stylistic statement. It should not be too obviously 1977."

Dean Anderson continued as a member of the group that met

regularly to review the progress of the design by Gerhard Kallmann and Michael McKinnell. Only one specific restraint was offered to the architects, most of whose previous buildings are celebrations of reinforced concrete. This rule was that there be no exposed concrete inside or out. "Of course not, we never would have considered it," Kallmann replied.

The academy, like most owners, came with several heads. The most influential one belonged to Dr. Edwin Land, chairman of the Polaroid Corporation, former president of the academy and the true begetter of its new building.

Land appeared only two or three times during the design stage but always with terrific impact. He expressed complete disdain for committees and groups of all kinds, although many such groups are sponsored by the academy. Instead he seemed to conceive of the academy as a maze of private nooks, off-stream backwaters where thinkers from different disciplines would meet casually to generate new ideas or, as he put it, places "where two great minds copulate."

"You need trysting places," he once said. "All I want is an even break for individualists. No group ever found the meaning of life." A physicist himself, he saw the academy as divided be-

---

Mr. Campbell is a practicing architect in Cambridge, Mass., and architectural critic for the *Boston Globe*.

tween physical scientists and social scientists, the former being individualists and the latter being natural group-formers. He wanted "secretive" access to private rooms, so that when two or three friends came to the new academy "they need not be confronted by huge symposia. You don't get a lot done in symposia."

Once Land delivered a memorable crit of the Ford Foundation headquarters in New York City. I've forgotten the words, but the gist was that everything is too harmonious at Ford. The real world, Land said, is a discord that is resolved only occasionally by talent. He felt that any attempt to create a world of apparent harmony was false and amounted to an affront to the creative spirit.

The layered, mazelike character of the academy ground floor plan, especially in the area of the so-called living rooms, is a direct response to this worthy client who knew what he liked and who clearly touched a sympathetic chord in the architects. Later, when Henry Milton, a member of the academy who is director of the Center for Advanced Study at the National Gallery of Art, saw the design, he said it looked like the plan of a

Exterior walls are of red brick trimmed in red granite, alternating with expanses of square glass panes framed in mahogany behind a procession of brick piers on the south and west. The project included restoration of the site as a park, partly for public use.

Mycenaean palace. When I passed this on to Kallmann he was delighted and quoted with relish an earlier comment by someone on Boston City Hall: "Not since Knossos have bureaucrats worked in such labyrinthine surroundings."

If Edwin Land was one major design determinant, the neighbors were another. The academy's lovely site was heir to a bitter history.

A house called Shady Hill once stood where the academy now stands, a house that was easily one of the half-dozen finest in Cambridge. In a remarkable act of cultural vandalism, Harvard abruptly demolished Shady Hill in August 1955 with the intention of redeveloping the site for dormitories. Outraged, the neighbors shot down a long series of Harvard schemes. Eventually the university gave up and offered the site to the academy.

To build at all, the academy needed a zoning variance, and in Cambridge this is obtainable only in the absence of serious opposition from neighbors. And at the start of its efforts the academy was faced with a petition of several hundred signatures opposing any construction on the site.

The process of persuading these people not to oppose the academy influenced its design dramatically. Their mere existence ensured that the building would be as polite as possible. More important, it was partly because of them that the building was moved from a shady, damp lower corner of the site—which

was all Harvard originally offered—up to the top of the knoll. This move caused a metamorphosis in the building.

On the lower site the building had been conceived as a kind of precinct. Columns inside the building were echoed by others standing free in the landscape. Indoor and outdoor space were equally part of the academy "grounds." It was fascinating to watch as the power of the new site gradually transformed the design from a precinct into a pavilion. It grew grander, more self-contained, until finally it became very much an object in space—the last thing the architects had originally intended. Soon they were talking of "a light sketch of a Tuscan villa." The notion the building now suggests—that it once was a more complete, pyramidal form that has been sliced back and chewed away—was arrived at by a series of intuitive adaptations to the new site, with the ideogram coming only afterward.

Because of these and other changes, the academy as built retains within its fabric the ghosts and marks of many design ideas that were abandoned along the way. This is surely one of its virtues. Isn't the difference between an original design like the academy and a mere knock-off precisely in the presence or absence of these ghosts of lost ideas? They give the original a depth, a slight inexplicability, that are absent in the copy. Because of them the finished building is the expression of a process, not of a single set of decisions, and gives the sense that time and change have washed over it even when it's brand new.

Kallmann and McKinnell have written persuasively of pastoral imagery and the notion of the building as a romantic ruin. Creation is mysterious, though, and sources are endless. Books by or about Kahn, MacKintosh, Aalto, Greene & Greene, and Voysey, and Girouard's *Sweetness and Light,* were all to be seen around the architects' office during design. Wright too is an obvious presence. Two modest sources that I can't help seeing in the building were never mentioned. One is a former stable in a Boston suburb, converted long since into a home for Thomas Adams, the academy treasurer. Its large sloping roof and long arcade of brick piers look very much like elements that appeared in the academy about the time of McKinnell's first visit to Adams's house. The other source, if it is one, is a conventional but attractive Tudor revival athletics building, next door to the Harvard swimming pool, where Kallmann swims three times a week. This has the academy's two-tiered roof, small-paned window-wall and, most strikingly, its frieze of large brackets beneath the eaves, here made of metal instead of wood.

I guess it's obvious, incidentally, that the academy's braces don't brace anything. Much of the building's visible structure, in fact, is rhetorical, a free variation on the underlying steel frame.

In my opinion the academy is best on its exterior, especially in the marvelous grace with which it rides the roll of the land. The landscape architect, Carol Johnson, as it happens, was often at odds with the architects. The conflict shows in a powerful building that seems to wish to radiate lines of force into the site, and a landscape that is not willing to be bowled over. It's a confrontation that is rather pleasing. Of the whole exterior only the great chimney seems to me to be slightly out of key, slightly overworked. Everything else is a triumph.

Indoors, the generally high level of success is undercut by a sense that things are too high and too grand. The atrium is so bright and strong that it tends to relegate the rooms around it to the status of periphery. The rooms are superb in themselves.

The staff offices upstairs are generous but pointlessly isolated from the public spaces below. There's a slightly distasteful sense of class in this, as if the bailiffs above must be kept from distracting the dukes strolling below.

The architects' concept for the furnishings was to acquire pieces (the academy owned almost nothing) that would be neither modern nor antique but simply traditional. These pieces would be chosen so as not quite to match, suggesting, for example, a sofa inherited from a grandmother that doesn't quite fit in but is too good not to use. This beguiling concept works

only partially, however, because the scale of the rooms is large enough to jar slightly with the domestic scale of the furnishings.

There have been practical problems—snow sliding off the roof, feedback in the audio, migrating upholstery in the lecture room—that have been very distracting to the owner but that perhaps don't amount to a great deal in the perspective of the building over time.

That perspective in any case is one I can't yet get into focus. The purpose of these notes is not to evaluate the architecture but only to offer fragments of one response and to keep alive some sense of the complexity and multiplicity of conditions that create any building in the last quarter of the 20th century.

To date, it appears the new academy is liked by everyone—by all the neighbors, who represent almost every social and cultural viewpoint, by the owner and by the architectural subculture itself—including this year's AIA jury, which gave it a national honor award. Given the moment in time at which it appeared, I think this breadth of appeal is its most difficult and important achievement. □

Steve Rosenthal

Donald Canty: Coming upon the academy building fresh, without having seen so much as a single photograph, it registers immediately as a place apart—which, of course, is one of the things it is intended to be. This serene pavilion on a wooded knoll could scarcely have less to do with the turbulent urban area in which, like it or not, it exists.

Its spiritual home might be Kyoto; or, more likely, the Adirondacks. In its luxuriant rusticity it would be quite at home in a millionaires' "camp" of other days. Gerhard Kallmann speaks of it in terms of "the idea of the country house" in England. But it is more like a lodge, a point curiously accentuated by the occasional use of bright green accents.

Moving from outside in, it quickly becomes apparent that the real apartness of this building is not spatial but temporal. It is a movement back into the 19th century—into rooms that might have been designed by the Greene brothers, the early Wright, any number of figures in what Kallmann terms the "premodern" period and mode.

This is historicism with a vengeance, but of a different sort than that associated with postmodernism. The latter's historical roots are sometimes classical, sometimes Corbusian, sometimes obscure, sometimes imaginary. Like modernism before it, postmodernism ignores or rejects the work of those remarkable architects of the last century who were crafting an architecture that was original, evocative and, in this country, particularly American. It was enticing, then, to hear of a major new work that set out to build upon these neglected beginnings, to reflect this rejected tradition.

It is a little disconcerting, however, to find that the academy's major rooms—a cluster of dining rooms, a pair of conference rooms, a drawing room, a library (using the term in the domestic sense rather than that of a place to store and dispense books) —are more recreations than reflections of the past. They do not

One of the dining rooms, typical of the interiors in its high ceilings, cove lighting, wood trim and use of 'grandmother's attic' furnishings. The dining rooms open to the atrium for extra capacity.

21

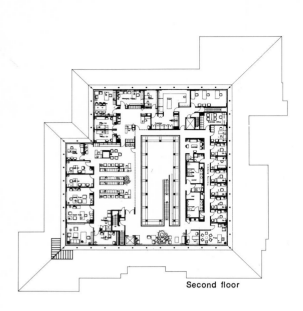

Second floor

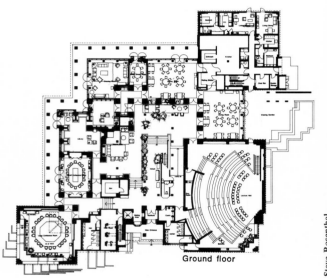

Ground floor

Steve Rosenthal

copy specific works, but except for a detail here and there they literally could have been done a century or so ago.

Let it be said, nevertheless, that these must be among the most beautiful rooms built anywhere in recent years. Ceilings rise to 14 feet, detailing is meticulous (and, as in the case of the fireplaces, imaginative), the use of materials sure-handed to the point of being loving. In the architects' words, "There is a consistent language of wainscotings, picture rails and framing of Honduras mahogany, surrounding painted or linen-covered fields."

The architects seem to have adopted some of the language of the period from which they draw. They speak of the ground level of the building as "a suite of rooms, entered from a skylit hall and hearth area," rooms that are "invested with inglenooks and window alcoves conducive to private encounter." This suite

Above, one of the two conference rooms. Across page above, the central atrium, flanked by scall parlors, with a draped skylight high overhead. At right, a second floor work space.

is a place of warmth and quiet and obvious seriousness, kept from gloominess by the constant presence of the garden.

The "skylit hall" or atrium is the meeting place of past and present, and here things begin to fall apart. Several different light fixtures are in view, including some on the wall that can only be called quaint; large ceramic urns, profusely planted, are distributed around the floor; the grand stairway bears an almost industrial-looking metal railing.

The stairway, and the space itself, imply a linkage between the first and second floors that does not exist in any important way. Downstairs is the scholars' suite, upstairs the domain of the staff, a set of pleasant but rather plain offices and auxiliary spaces, perhaps seeming plainer than they might elsewhere because of the contrast with the moments of magnificence below.

Likewise, if the building somehow disappoints it might be because of arriving at it with exaggerated expectations. After all, the architects have positively augmented the sensitive site, have given their clients exactly what they wanted—and there are those stirring moments in the 19th century rooms. □

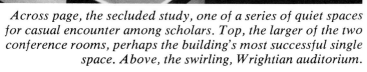

Across page, the secluded study, one of a series of quiet spaces for casual encounter among scholars. Top, the larger of the two conference rooms, perhaps the building's most successful single space. Above, the swirling, Wrightian auditorium.

The study's highly ornamented fireplace, one of three on the academy's ground floor, is of red granite framed in wood.

Geometry in the Service of Society

William Kessler's Coleman Young Recreation Center, Detroit. By Stanley Abercrombie, AIA

Balthazar Korab

Photographs by Balthazar Korab

The best-seller list may be crowded these days with such books as *How to Do the Cube,* but William Kessler doesn't need to read them. His Detroit firm has developed skills for manipulating cubes and other modules in ways that Rubik never imagined. Such modularity has sometimes been synonymous with structure, as in the 1975 Center for Creative Studies, sometimes not, as in the honor-award-winning Wayne State University Health Care Institute (mid-May 1980). In either case, according to Kessler, "The design module is something we have been pursuing for a long time—not at all to the point of creating an inflexible grid, but to give us a sort of matrix within which we can play."

But if such preoccupations suggest a dry estheticism or a removal from problems of site, function and social responsibility, forget the suggestion. The building we show here, for example, the recently completed Coleman Young Recreation Center, is a geometric extravaganza indeed, but one completely in the service of its users, a "play" within a "matrix," but one finely tuned to the demands of a confusing context, a strangely shaped site, a complex program, a prospect of rough usage and a tight budget. It provides ingeniously interlocking facilities for physical recreation; simultaneously, it provides a generous amount of visual recreation and spatial sport; and these provisions reinforce each other to produce a whole that is more—and more fun—than the sum of its parts.

The context of the Coleman Young center, within walking distance of Detroit's downtown, is one of the country's largest (500 acres), earliest (1951) and slowest to be completed (almost, but not quite yet) urban renewal efforts. Once called the Gratiot Redevelopment Area, it moved a major step forward in 1954 when the Citizens' Redevelopment Corporation, organized by Walter Reuther and others, commissioned a master plan by Oscar Stonorov, Victor Gruen Associates, and Leinweber, Yamasaki & Hellmuth. Another major step was the completion in 1959 and 1960 of the Lafayette Park section of the site, with

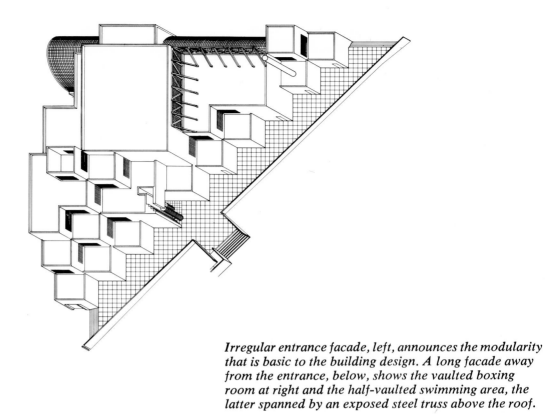

Irregular entrance facade, left, announces the modularity that is basic to the building design. A long facade away from the entrance, below, shows the vaulted boxing room at right and the half-vaulted swimming area, the latter spanned by an exposed steel truss above the roof.

30

Major spaces under soaring glass block vaults.

apartment slabs and town houses designed by Mies van der Rohe. At present, construction continues in the Elmwood Park portion, just east of Lafayette Park, and it is a critical site at the heart of Elmwood Park that was assigned to the recreation center.

A basic design decision was to place straight building edges along two perpendicular street lines and to present a more irregular facade to the curving approach road, Elmwood Park's major new thoroughfare. It was originally hoped that the irregularities would be filled, in part, by the addition of small shops, thus intensifying the building's role as a community center, but this remains only a hope.

Despite its irregularities, the entrance wall has been given a definite focus, an entrance delightfully elaborated with stepping surfaces, flying beams resting on glass block cylinders (with lighting inside, as well as structure) and a display of square grids at various scales—all serving as introductions to the interior. A further exterior hint of interior effects is given by a glimpse of enormous exposed roof trusses, painted bright green; obviously, some spaces here must expand beyond the apparent module.

Inside, there are large spaces indeed: a gymnasium, a boxing ring, a swimming pool and two handball courts. There are also many smaller spaces, of course, for meetings, arts and crafts, ceramics and photography. Except for one long hall wrapping around the locker rooms, corridors have been minimized, most

The swimming area's half-vault, left, is of 12x12-inch glass block, as is the full vault over the boxing ring, above. In the gymnasium, below, truss is visible through glass block clerestory.

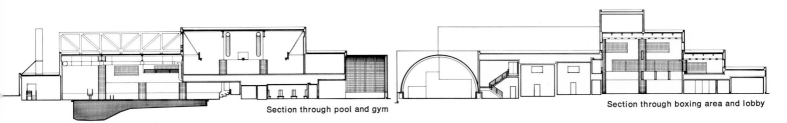

Section through pool and gym

Section through boxing area and lobby

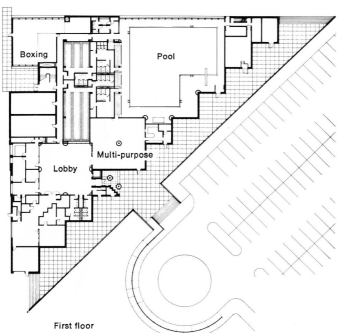

Boxing

Pool

Multi-purpose

Lobby

First floor

Second floor corridor, above, steps out in small alcoves that will have tables and chairs for games. Beyond the glass block screen is the main lobby, right, a double height space enlivened by cylinders of glass block and dry-wall grids at two different scales.

A consistent palette and pervasive modularity.

circulation spaces doubling as lobby area or game areas. All these, along with offices, locker rooms and necessary service areas, have been orchestrated into a comprehensible whole by means of a striking but limited color range—gray, black, the soft brown of the ground face block used both inside and out, and a brilliant green—and of the all-pervading modularity.

The most basic of the modules in use here is a 24x24-foot structural and planning grid. An overscale lattice hung between floors in the double-height lobby, serving no function except to modulate the space in a fascinating way, is on an 8x8-foot grid, and the ceiling grid a level above, concealing electrical and mechanical services, is of 4x4-foot squares. Wood block flooring is of 6x6-inch squares; ceramic tiles are 1x1-inch square, and there are squares and double squares as well in the ground face block and glass block. Naturally, without a large budget for custom fixtures, there have been a few details that have escaped alignment (fire hose cabinets remain recalcitrant), but it is extraordinary that the grid has been applied so consistently. Perhaps it is this thorough modularity that lends such a feeling of release to the areas in the building that are too big to conform. The sense of openness is further enhanced in the boxing area by a vault of glass block and in the swimming area by a half vault (its column-free junction, over the pool, with a flat ceiling plane being a bit alarming until we remember those big green roof trusses).

"Euclid alone has looked on Beauty bare," Edna St. Vincent Millay told us. Maybe so, but William Kessler has given a whole Detroit community a near-Euclidian glimpse of Her. □

Corporate Campus Laid Back Against Telegraph Hill

Hellmuth, Obata & Kassabaum's Levi's Plaza, San Francisco. By D.C.

L evi's Plaza in San Francisco may be absolutely unique as a corporate headquarters. Others have taken on a campus plan with low buildings arranged around landscaped open spaces, such as the urbane plaza and informal park here. But none has been built on quite such an urban, and urbane, site as these four blocks at the base of flavorful Telegraph Hill facing the Embarcadero.

Behind it is an unusual company and an unusual history. Levi Strauss was born as a supplier of jeans to the miners of the California gold rush, whose demands were unusually rugged. By the way time is measured in the West it is an old San Francisco company, in the hands of one of the city's more benevolent old families. "It is the kind of family," says HOK-San Francisco's William Valentine, "where they gave the patriarch, Walter Haas Sr., a park for his birthday every year," dedicating a piece of open space to public use in his name.

Until the 1970s Levi Strauss headquarters was an aging five-story building on Battery Street near the Embarcadero. Then came explosive growth when jeans became big business world-wide and the company diversified to the point where its annual sales approached some $2 billion.

Outgrowing its old headquarters, the company moved to one of the towers of John Portman's Embarcadero Center. But it wasn't the same, according to Robert D. Haas, the company's current chief executive. Highrise quarters brought more hierarchical stratification, and the old chances for informal contact

between strata and between parts of the company were gone. More important, says Haas, so was "the spirit of Battery Street," which he defines as an almost family-like closeness.

At the same time, a developer named Gerson Bakar had acquired the four blocks at the base of the hill and was making his plans for them. Bakar was best known to the local architectural community as client for the early classic Woodlake garden apartment development in San Mateo designed by William W. Wurster.

Bakar had worked with HOK and Arthur Gensler & Associates in the past and asked both to come up with proposals for the site. He chose HOK's scheme and Gensler subsequently was put in charge of the interiors. It was a polite, lowrise scheme, partly because of the architects' and client's proclivities, and partly because some very powerful and vocal residents of Telegraph Hill were breathing right down the backs of their necks.

Bakar heard of Levi Strauss's restiveness and approached them. At first they took part of the space and later all, with Bakar assuming their Embarcadero Center lease. At that point Robert Haas entered the design process, along with Howard Friedman, the company's architectural consultant, and landscape architect Lawrence Halprin.

The main plaza is defined by two new round-cornered buildings and a remodeled warehouse. Its paving continues downward across Battery Street to the lower level park. The photo above was taken from one of the other two new buildings at park level.

36

Italian Swiss
Colony Warehouse

Office building

Office building

Office building

The Embarcadero

Cargo West

Four new buildings, and two old, on two parcels.

The design that emerged from these various hands is basically simple but full of complexities, wonders and a few contradictions. The site is bisected by Battery, of all streets, into a two block rectangle to the west, directly under the hill along Sansome Street, and a triangle of like size between it and the Embarcadero. Pre-existing were Cargo West, a little brick treasure where sailors were often shanghaied during San Francisco's even more hedonist days, and a handsome Italian Swiss Colony wine warehouse, on the southeast and northeast corners of the rectangle.

Both were retained and remodeled and joining them on the rectangle are two new buildings of five and seven stories, the latter the quarters of top Levi Strauss management, with a soaring glass atrium framed in blue-painted steel as its lobby. The same denim blue is used as trim elsewhere.

The buildings partly enclose a large plaza bearing an exceptional Halprin fountain, with a wide opening toward the water and a narrower one looking up Telegraph Hill to its landmark, Coit Tower.

The triangle bears two additional office buildings joined at third story level by a bridge. The rest of its space is given over to a park designed by Halprin as "an abstraction of a water course in the Sierras" where the company found its first customers. The park contains a smaller fountain and also a meandering stream.

Parking for the complex is across Sansome Street, underneath a condominium being developed by Bakar. From it to the fountain a two-story colonade has been cut through the smaller of the two office buildings on the rectangle, providing a moment of genuine drama. Along the colonade, and on the ground floors of this building and the old warehouse facing the plaza, will be shops and restaurants. The atrium of the largest office building also is programmed for extensive public use, with a third-story balcony projecting out into the space for musical and other performances and, presumably, oratory.

There is also less well-used access to the plaza from the Sansome side down a handsome set of wide steps axial to its midpoint. From here, as Halprin puts it, there is a two-way tug to the fountain, the "public" side of the plaza, and the headquarters building, the corporate side.

Major foot traffic also enters the complex from the Ferry

So congenial is Levi's Plaza to its surroundings that it almost disappears among them. To find it, ascribe a line straight down to the right from Coit Tower atop the hill.

Photographs by Joshua Freiwald

Above, the colonnade from Sansome Street. Right, the bridge between the two triangle buildings. Across page, the Halprin fountain in the main plaza, looking across Battery Street to the park and Embarcadero.

Pedestrian paths and spaces—and lots of brick.

Building side beneath the bridge linking the two buildings on the triangle. From here those headed for the plaza forge across Battery Street. A bridge between the two parcels, either from ground level or overhead, as between the triangle buildings, never was seriously considered. Halprin for one says he would have opposed a lower bridge because it would have blocked views from the plaza to the bay. But without some linkage the complex remains visually and functionally bisected.

It is unified to some degree by the form and materials of the new buildings. They are built of precast brick on 30-foot panels whose width set the design module (followed also in the plaza paving). Where used full width the panels have glazed openings in the shape of inverted, truncated "U"s, giving them a configuration intended to recall San Francisco's traditional bay windows.

The buildings' most distinctive characteristic is the "carving away" of the corners, as Valentine puts it. They step back one bay per floor, softening the form and creating exceedingly pleasant triangular balconies. About half of these balconies open from executive offices, and the other half, democratically, from

Top photos, the atrium of the main building, from the plaza and from inside. Right, ground level view of the upper fountain. Far right, a view across one of the corner terraces.

Photographs by Joshua Freiwald

A series of varied experiences, inside and out.

lounges and other employee facilities. The views in all directions are spectacular.

From the outset the open spaces in the project were considered as important as the buildings. The spaces vary markedly in every way. The upper one is somewhat formal, even harsh (an impression that may be due in part to its newness). But this plaza has a wonderful off-center centerpiece in the Halprin fountain. It has many sitting levels and steps for walking in and around it, water goes in a variety of directions—and it is topped by a huge granite boulder of a powerful, irregular shape that Halprin found in the Sierras. It looks, as he intended, as if it had "rolled down Telegraph Hill" and landed in the plaza.

The fountain below (overleaf) is similar enough to one above to seem a pale quotation of it. This one is not so much intended for walking in and around its courses. Rather it is a turning point in a path by the stream that is intended to carefully guide the stroller to the best views of the water. The opening between piers here is the only such break on this stretch of the Embarcadero.

Along the stream and on the slopes beside it are a seemingly random assortment of rocks and boulders. Each was carefully chosen by Halprin, however, and precisely positioned in drawings of the park.

It is, in a way, symbolic of the carefully staged romanticism that has much to do with the success of Levi's Plaza—and of the city in which it has been built. □

Lawrence Halprin

Joshua Freiwald

Right, the lower fountain and the beginning of the stream through the park. Grassy knoll (top) is sunk well below the level of surrounding streets. Above, the warehouse from the park.

Joshua Freiwald

The Wainwright:
Building on Genius

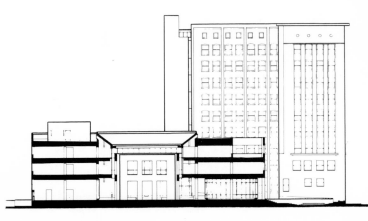

Mitchell/Giurgola's restoration of and additions to Louis Sullivan's Wainwright Building, St. Louis.
By Stanley Abercrombie, AIA

Above and right, two views of the Wainwright with its addition. Top right, a section through the midblock courtyard of the addition. In site plan, below, original building is shaded.

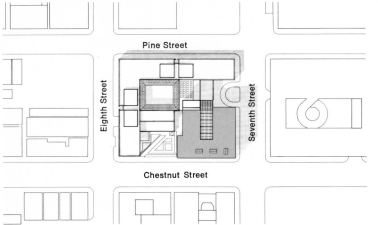

Writing in the 1924 *Architectural Record* about the late Louis Sullivan, Frank Lloyd Wright remembered it this way: "When he brought in the board with the motive of the Wainwright Building outlined in profile and in scheme upon it and threw it down on my table, I was perfectly aware of what had happened. This was Louis Sullivan's greatest moment —his greatest effort. The 'skyscraper' as a new thing under the sun, an entity with virtue, individuality and beauty all its own, was born."

Yet 50 years later, this "greatest effort," this building that had shown the way to an appropriate architecture for the tall office block, lay derelict. Without tenants, without landmark status, a liability to its owner, it was in imminent danger, in the early '70s, of being replaced by a parking lot—and this in the heart of St. Louis, a city whose heart needs nothing less than it needs another parking lot.

It was the National Trust for Historic Preservation that came to the rescue at the last moment (late 1973) with a gesture unprecedented in the trust's history: it bought a nine-month option on the property. With no experience as a developer or landlord, the trust found itself with a threatened landmark of its very own. But almost at the same time it was becoming clear that there was a need in St. Louis for a centralized location for state offices; Governor Christopher S. Bond sought and won from the Missouri General Assembly an appropriation for a building that would house 18 different agencies then in leased quarters scattered around the city; and in 1974 the Wainwright was designated for the purpose. A national competition was held for a design that would renovate the 1891 building's 150,000 square feet of office space and add 100,000 square feet of new construction. The winners, announced in November 1974, were Mitchell/ Giurgola of New York and Philadelphia with Hastings & Chivetta of St. Louis. Budget problems and disagreements about the most advantageous bidding procedures delayed the start of construction until 1978, but it was finally completed last June and dedicated by Governor Bond (who, in the meantime, had been defeated, then subsequently re-elected) as the Wainwright State Office Building.

Sullivan's original building was U-shaped, its office wings wrapped around an interior light well. The new design adds a glass roof to the light well, making it an interior atrium and allowing removal of glass in all the windows facing into it, and adds three lower L-shaped structures that edge the rest of the block and enclose new courtyards. The competition entry proposed terminating the open end of the light well with a bank of new elevators, but, at the suggestion of historian Vincent Scully, a competition juror, this bank has been shifted to the end of one of the original wings, and the end of the atrium has also been glazed, with new connecting bridges at each floor. Interior hallways of the original building have been moved to the perimeter of the atrium, providing a newly sunny, pleasant circulation pattern and larger, more flexible office areas than before. The atrium

Aluminum entrance 'improvements,' below, have been restored to original appearance, right. One end of the former light well, newly enclosed as an atrium, bottom, is roofed by an original canopy of stained glass. The other end, right, has new glazing and connecting bridges at each floor.

Stanley Abercrombie, AIA

Sadin/Karant

Augmenting a landmark, inside and out.

floor reproduces the ceramic tile pattern originally used in the entrance lobby, and an original stained glass canopy, stored during construction (and, for a while, thought to be either lost or stolen) has been reused at one end of the atrium.

The new elements of the composition have been arranged so that they retain the distinctive quadrant division of the city block typical for this section of St. Louis: New circulation paths align with former service alleys, providing some unexpected visual links to neighboring blocks. And the building masses have not only been related in appropriately subsidiary ways to the original building; they have also been disposed so as to form three new ground-level pedestrian areas, each with a character of its own. The most formal of these is the one nearest the new elevator tower. Open to the street along one edge, it provides a vehicular entrance for ceremonial occasions (closed to vehicles most of the time by bollards and chains) and, beyond a screen of brick pierced with window-scaled openings, a fountain and pool.

A channel of water, sunk into the paving, takes the water from this pool into the second courtyard. This one, in the center of the block, is surrounded on all sides by new construction, but paths along two edges lead directly to surrounding streets, and the construction here is sufficiently ambiguous to dispel any feeling of close confinement. Four walls of granite are split apart at their corners and are separated as well from the actual building faces a few feet behind them. Solid masonry is here treated as a freestanding screen in front of a building volume, which, faced with reflective glass and aluminum, mirrors the screen beyond it. At the center of this courtyard, the water channel creates a small circular pool and leaves it again at right angles, traveling on, curving round an apsidal glazed exhibition area, through a "moon gate" in another brick wall, to the third outdoor area.

This space, also open along one side to the street, is domi-

46

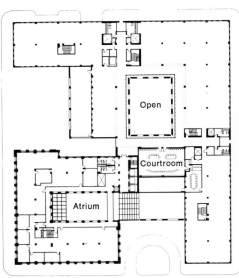

Third floor

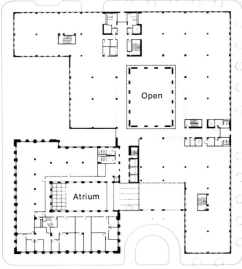

Second floor

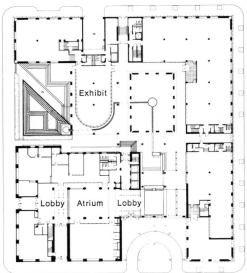

Ground floor

In the midblock courtyard, right, a water channel forms a small pool and changes direction. Granite screens are held away from the actual building walls beyond. At top, the third floor circulation space around the courtyard. Above, a skylighted courtroom on the third floor.

Photographs by Sadin/Karant

A loner made part of a new composition.

nated by a large triangular pool, the final destination of the water channel. Level changes within the pool add visual interest and, when the water is drained for winter months, can be used for seating. This courtyard, like the first, allows maximum exposure of the Wainwright's off-street wall areas that received the same decorative treatment as the street faces. (Farther into the block, a plainer treatment was expedient for wall surfaces never meant to be seen.)

Thus the Wainwright, originally quite a loner, has been incorporated into a complex, ingenious, delightful new composition covering the whole block. Unfortunately, a small measure of that delight may be in danger: The water channel, which works so well to enliven and relate the three courtyards, has proved to be a hazard for people who don't watch where they're walking,

and, when seen last fall, was temporarily covered here and there with sheets of plywood. The Mitchell/Giurgola office has submitted a proposal for covering some of the channels with granite bridges and for placing new benches and planters so as to prevent further accidents, but resolution of the problem is uncertain.

Successfully related as old and new construction may be here —in color, in general scale, in relationships of void to solid— the new buildings have a distinctive character of their own. It derives from the use of certain currently fashionable architectural mannerisms. These are mannerisms that can seem merely nervous jitters in the hands of lesser designers, but that Romaldo Giurgola handles confidently—unexpected cuttings, screenings and layerings, surprising contrasts, intriguing ambiguities. In this particular building group, these serve a particular need, for, not in quality but in quantity, there is less building here than meets the eye. A minimum amount of building mass was neces-

49

Cooperation between new and old—and agencies.

sary to convincingly complete the Wainwright block, and one infers that the building program called for something less than that minimum. The screen walls, the enclosed roof terraces, the false fronts in this case provide the needed illusion. If such a formal vocabulary had not already existed, it might well have been invented for this design.

But new construction here is only half the story (measured by dollars, almost exactly half the $14 million cost). The rest of the story, of course, is the restoration of the Adler & Sullivan skyscraper. Perhaps the most striking aspect of the restoration is the building's cleaning and consequent color change from the sooty maroon seen by pilgrims of recent decades to the bright rosy red that it once was and is again. Many parts of the building were cleaned and repaired, some (such as hardware), partly missing, were matched with new copies where necessary, and some details, considered irreparable, were replaced with new construction. One of these was the cornice projecting at the level of the third floor sills, along the line where the building's sandstone base changes to brick: This cornice could not be saved, so a new one was constructed of sandstone quarried in Germany (to match the original sandstone quarried in Michigan but no longer available); its top surface is protected by a sheet of tern-coated stainless steel to prevent recurrence of the deterioration. Wood entrance doors, similar to the originals, have replaced the aluminum "improvements," and, throughout the building, there are now new window frames of teak matching the original ones of red cypress. The facade restoration was assisted by a grant from the U.S. Department of Housing and Urban Development.

Which brings us to another admirable aspect of the Wainwright story. It is a manifestation not only of new design cooperating with old, but also of several federal agencies cooperating with several state ones. As Carleton Knight III wrote in the National Trust's *Preservation News,* "Others please copy." □

Above, the composition of old and new seen from the north. Right, an exterior wall split at the traditional location of a midblock alley. Far right, the triangular pool at the end of the water channel's course.

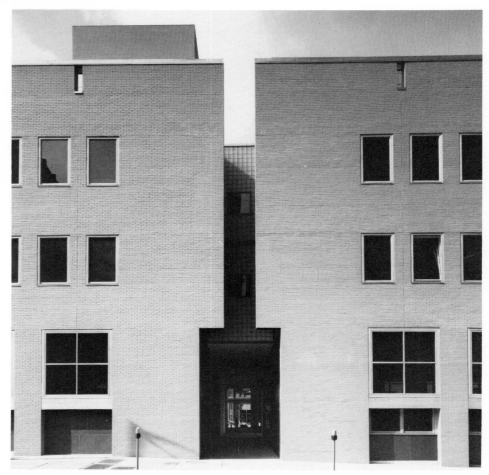

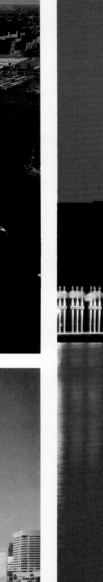

Another Powerful Harborside Attraction

The Cambridge Seven's National Aquarium in Baltimore. By Nora Richter Greer

A dramatic building on a dramatic site, this is the newest attraction at Baltimore's thriving Inner Harbor and has been so successful that it had to be closed for 10 days in March for minor refurbishing after only five months of operation.

Originally the aquarium was to be sited along the shoreline. Fortunately it was pushed out to the end of a pier jutting into the harbor, giving it a presence matched only by the massive old power plant to its north. The pier location allowed the building to become a "symbol or expression of reaching out to sea," in the words of Peter Chermayeff, Cambridge Seven principal in charge. The thrusting effect is mainly achieved by a glass pyramid at the building's prow, "a pointed form with some directional

shape that came very early [in the design process] as a gesture of looking seaward," Chermayeff continues.

The large pyramid shelters a tropical rain forest and is repeated as a canopy over the entrance. Both are echoed by a bright-orange pipe sculpture located next to the small pyramid. The two pyramids sit atop the building's concrete base; on the western facade the area underneath them is smooth plywood-formed concrete painted a deep blue to articulate the glass forms and

The aquarium at night from across the harbor, above. Located on a pier, the building symbolically thrusts out to sea (facing page, above). In lower photo, opposite, the unadorned eastern facade.

Moving upward through a dazzling space.

give them a base, according to Chermayeff. To create a festive image, the blue panels are decorated with brightly colored squares resembling signal flags. While this western facade reflects the "recreational" image of the harbor, the eastern one is more sober in its unadorned concrete with minimal fenestration.

Visitors enter the building by ascending stairs under the small pyramid to the lobby amid the sight and sound of bubbling water, and once inside are held on a carefully choreographed one-directional route. The first stop is by a huge tank of dolphins. From there movement is upward by escalators passing through

a dramatic central volume to three floors of exhibitions. Most of the exhibitions line darkened perimeter hallways with small tanks of fish and accompanying texts describing the aquatic animals and their environment (the exhibits illustrate schooling, evolving, hiding, growing, feeding, moving, lurking; how fish swim, eat, evolve).

The drama is heightened by sounds of marine life, color transparencies flashed on the walls, views down to the dolphins frolicking in their pool, peeks into the shark and coral reef tanks, a neon wave superimposed upon the wall of the main space and a 24-foot-long whale skeleton hanging from the ceiling.

As a climax to and a relief from the dazzle of the exhibition

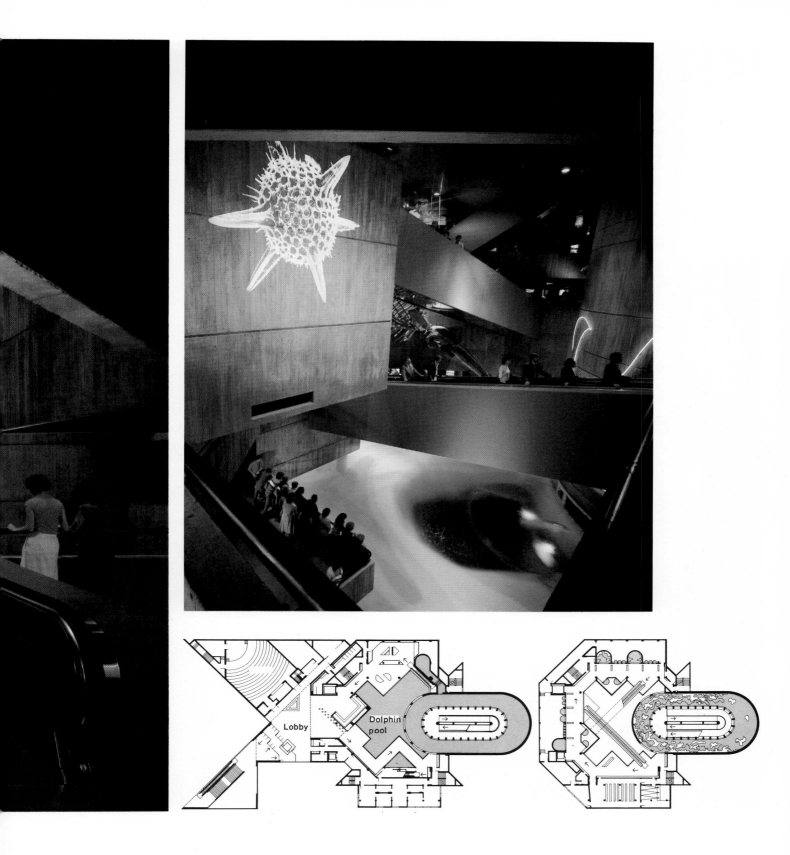

floors, the final escalator leads upward into the tropical rain forest, 64 feet high at its apex. It offers a peaceful setting, interrupted only by the sounds of live animals and simulated lightning. On a clear day, it also provides magnificent views of Harborplace and the city beyond.

From the rain forest, the visitor descends by carpeted ramps, surrounded by cavernous oblong fish tanks. The upper one represents a coral reef, and the lower one is inhabited by countless

In the dramatic central space escalators criss-cross above the dolphin pool located on the first floor, and a neon wave decorates the oblong-shaped fish tanks, photos above and drawings.

sharks. The ramps were made wide enough for wheelchairs, and the trip down them contrasts with the experience of the tight passageways of the exhibition spaces. And then the final surprise. Upon leaving the shark tank, the visitor again sees the dolphins, by now long forgotten, gliding through their underwater environment. A final educational message comes from the man in the sea exhibit, meant to "provoke" the visitors to "some kind of consciousness of our responsibility" to protect the world's ecosystems.

Since Cambridge Seven designed the building and the exhibits simultaneously, the result is a thoroughly integrated interior where the edges between the exhibits and the architecture are

Moving downward through huge fish tanks.

blurred. It is, in all, an exciting and instructive experience. But it is a carefully controlled one.

When the museum is crowded, and it usually is, the darkened, small exhibit halls seem cramped. And a visitor cannot retrace his steps and may even be hurried along by a push from behind. Occasional feelings of claustrophobia are alleviated, however, by the periodic release into the central space.

Chermayeff chose the nondetouring path for two reasons:

to get more efficient use out of a small amount of space (and in the process, more out of a tight budget) and to orchestrate the entire show as an "experience in a way that is really not unlike that in a film or in a book," with a clear beginning, climax, release and conclusion. Cambridge Seven used this type of circulation system previously in its celebrated New England aquarium

Under the larger glass pyramid, 64 feet high at its apex, is the tropical rain forest, left. At the top of the tanks, views into the coral reef, above. The two tanks surround descending ramps.

in Boston (whose ramps encircle the perimeter of a great central tank) and in the exhibits in the U.S. pavilion at Montreal's Expo '67.

Chermayeff points out that the design obviates the need for large spaces to accommodate two-way traffic, as in more traditional museums, where visitors randomly wander. "If you get into a random pattern," Chermayeff says, "you tend to find that people really look on the museum not as an experience but as an assemblage of random encounters that may or may not hold together for them." □

Sculptural Shapes That Sit Solidly on the Ground

Hugh Newell Jacobsen's Gettysburg, Pa., College Library.
By Andrea Oppenheimer Dean

Photographs by Balthazar Korab

This building is peculiar in some ways, extraordinary in others and full of surprises. Few would guess, to begin with, that the architect is Hugh Newell Jacobsen, FAIA. He is known for his elegant, refined houses, usually white with simple, retiring geometric shapes. By contrast, this 73,000-square-foot, five-story building at Gettysburg College in southern Pennsylvania is a tough and muscular-looking building (aptly named Musselman Library). It is Jacobsen's first institutional building in the U.S. and rises in burgundy brick and tinted precast concrete coursing topped by gabled slate roofs from a four-foot concrete base that flares as it hits the ground. Horizontal, glazed openings in the base bring light into an English-style basement. Above it are three floors of reading rooms, stacks and administrative offices. The space under the roof contains mechanical services.

The building's squat, sculptural shapes, and even its plan, look as though they might have been invented by an imaginative Druid. On the south elevation, as one approaches the building from the main road, an apsidal-shaped reading room slips away from the main rectangle of the structure. It is scored with floor-to-ceiling slits of glazing (unmanned by gunners); narrow slashes of glass also mount the peaked roof. Entrance to the building is from the northwest corner through glazed openings that pivot around a huge, round stair tower cum campanile. It is the building's only unbroken vertical, and reminds one of shapes pre-medieval, Mendelsohnian, and also of grain elevators and industrial smokestacks. On the west facade are three glazed bays that house carrel-like spaces. On the east, a wall slips out to form a courtyard; visually, this elevation is dominated by a smaller tower and great expanses of black roofing. As Jacobsen says, "There is a lot going on here in terms of architecture, the slipped apsidal shape, the funny tower, the very Italianate campanile."

The stated reason for Musselman Library's shapes, materials and colors was to create a building "that is polite to the neighbors, like a well-mannered lady," in Jacobsen's words. The neighbors are rather prim but sweet-looking Georgian structures. The exceptions are a humanities building of fairly recent vintage and, as jewel of the campus, a late 19th century Richardsonian Romanesque structure called Glatfelter Hall. Jacobsen's principal charge was to create a companion for Glatfelter, compatible but late 20th century in form and spirit.

But even before it took form in bricks and mortar, the new structure was physically moved away from its companion-to-be. A major donor to the library attached to a large monetary gift the condition that the site and placement be changed to avoid destroying an existing structure and venerable old trees.

In its original position, the new library would have been farther than it now is from the main street, partially screened from it by another building, and would have presented one of its quieter, long elevations to the road. Its apsidal reading room would have faced east and its shape would have followed a half-circular path separating it from Glatfelter while echoing Glatfelter's rounded corner bay. But Musselman was pulled south and east, away from Glatfelter. Its axis was rotated, and its plan reversed, requiring some 40 working drawings to be redone in mirror image.

So, today as one approaches the library from the road, its shape looms. The building is separated from Glatfelter by a small Georgian structure, and it requires several 180-degree turns of the head to recognize that the library's north facade is an abstraction of Glatfelter's south elevation in reverse.

Unlike the surrounding Georgian fabric of the campus, finely grained, carefully articulated and looking like a series of bas-relief carvings, Musselman is a freestanding creation, different on all sides. Its broad shapes, though visually cordoned off from

Above left, Musselman Library from the south with Glatfelter Hall's tower in the background; left, a view of the west elevation with carrel-like, glazed spaces. Above right, the north-facing entrance; right, the original site plan, and far right, as built.

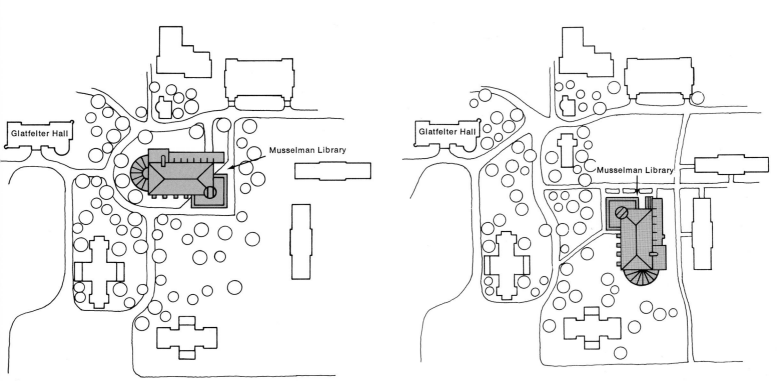

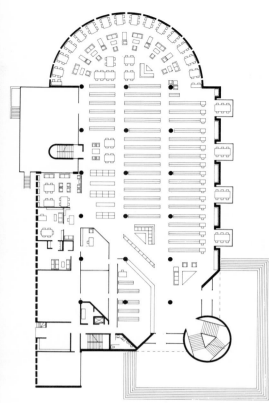

'An agile and inventive use of light.'

one another, are mostly horizontal, continuous and smooth, almost without texture, differing both from its Georgian neighbors and Glatfelter, with its humanizing bumps and warts. And in contrast to the Gettysburg campus colors—red, white, gray and black—the new library is essentially two-tone—black on top, shades of red below.

The surprising thing is that Musselman Library's unlikely confabulation of hefty forms displays many of the hallmarks of Jacobsen's houses after all. There is the adroit and picturesque massing, the formal sense of order, the scrupulously careful, beautiful detailing, And, big and fat as it is, Musselman Library is still elegant.

The interior is even more immediately and recognizably vintage Jacobsen. There is the expected, uninterrupted flow of spaces, the agile, inventive use of light (floor-to-ceiling glazing in various configurations, plus skylights and clerestories), the familiar, clean, unfussy lines and straight juxtaposed to curved surfaces.

But here too the building is full of surprises. The first is that the interior feels much smaller than expected, much lighter and airier. The two entranceways are separated by the massive stair tower, which exists not only to echo Glatfelter's campanile but to be climbed. And what a climb, on broad risers with exquisitely detailed railing, toward the light—and incidentally to three floors of stacks. The elevator is purposely hidden away to discourage its use.

The main portion of the building is given over to an almost rectangular reading room at grade, stacks on upper floors. The module was determined by the distance between fluorescent strips (four feet, six inches apart) that, contrary to what is typical for libraries, run on a diagonal of 45 degrees. This allows greater flexibility of layout, plus a livelier, more ample-seeming

The apsidal reading room with its dramatic, natural lighting, left and right, flows into a larger, rectangular space. Above, the interior as seen from the entrance and the first floor plan.

On the west elevation, left and below, are glazed study alcoves, each with a table and four chairs plus an individual desk. A slanted skylight and careful detailing make the stairwell, right, a dramatic and welcoming space.

Functions clearly deliniated and expressed.

space. Brick-covered columns march along on center 25 feet, six inches apart.

On the east side of the building, where the wall juts out to create an enclosed courtyard at grade level, there are, as one moves south, first glazed offices, then a glassed-in reading room and, before reaching the apsidal end space, a smaller stair tower surrounded by green. Four glazed rooms, each containing a table and four chairs plus an individual desk and chair, protrude on the west side of the library. The unfortunate exposure to afternoon sun is another consequence of having changed the position of the building. The original plan would have given these spaces a southern exposure.

Facing south now is the curved, light-filled reading room. It is a virtuoso performance, especially in its use of natural illumination. Floor-to-ceiling slits display glimpses of the outside; and sweeping slashes up the half-cone of the two story wall/ceiling give a sense of daring, of something uplifting and rousing in spirit. The mood here is gayer, more cheerful than in the principal reading room, and colors look brighter, clearer.

Especially in this space it is clear how much Jacobsen remains the modernist, despite flights into fantasy and history. Spaces and functions are clearly marked off from one another without any blurring of edges. Structure and functions are expressed; there is no add-on ornament, and no element exists without functional justification. □

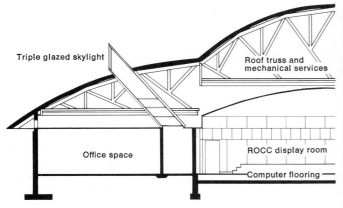

Triple glazed skylight

Roof truss and mechanical services

Office space

ROCC display room

Computer flooring

Photographs by Larry Pacilio

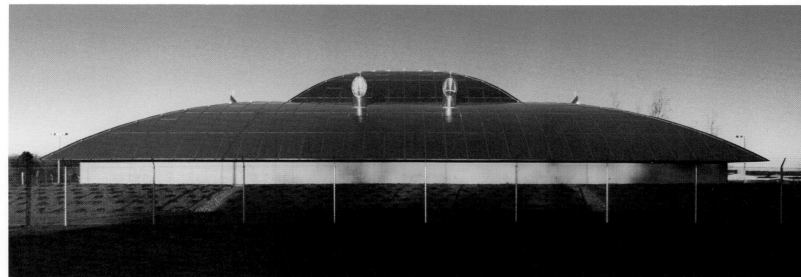

Curving Canopy of Gleaming Metal

Stetson/Dale's Griffiss Air Force Base operations center, Rome, N.Y. By S.A.

Griffiss Air Force Base, Rome, N.Y., is a collection of diverse utilitarian buildings, some distinguished by paint colors that manage to be simultaneously garish and murky, most not distinguished in any way, all littered about the landscape without discernible evidence of human intelligence; it is not a likely place to look for architecture. The base's new ROCC (Region Operations Control Center) building has a plan predetermined for the architects by the military, and supervision of its construction was not in the hands of the architects but of the U.S. Navy, which provides such services for the Air Force; not a likely set of circumstances to nurture architecture. And ROCC's designer, except for that floor plan, was Stetson/Dale of nearby Utica, a large (180-person) architecture-engineering firm with more engineers—structural, mechanical, electrical, civil—than architects; not the type of firm, conventional wisdom says, most likely to produce innovative design.

Yet Stetson/Dale, by interpreting the rigid program literally and considering the harsh climate thoughtfully, has designed a

remarkably strong and imaginative building. It is almost enough to make one believe that form should follow function.

ROCC's function, specifically, is to house men and equipment for a key part of the country's air surveillance system. There are three other such units in the continental U.S., two in Canada, another in Alaska, all based on that same plan; together they receive and monitor data from 46 radar sites, providing information about all aircraft approaching North America. All other considerations were secondary to the imperative one of keeping this activity secure and dry, and, for that reason, there were to be no windows and no internal roof drains (which might freeze and then leak). Additional program requirements were that the building reduce energy consumption by 45 percent relative to a similar facility built five years earlier (a reduction of 53 percent was actually achieved) and that design criteria established by the Navy, the Air Force, the Occupational Safety and Health Administration and the Department of Defense all be observed.

Basic design decisions, according to Donald Wilhelm, project

Glowing 'snouts' and color-coded interiors.

architect for Stetson/Dale, included the use of energy-conserving earth berms against perimeter walls and a vaulted roof of aluminum sheeting that curves down nearly to the berm and provides efficient drainage of rain and snow. The small amount of vertical wall is shielded from the sun by a generous overhang, and the soffit of this overhang provides space for air intakes, toilet vents and other mechanical equipment that would normally have penetrated the roof surface. It is all eminently sensible, and demonstrably so (Stetson/Dale had to prove, for example, that the curved roof form was no more expensive than a shed roof would be), but it is, happily, more than that. The great shiny vault, its shape emphasized by the standing seams between aluminum panels, is suitably technological in character, yet also repeats the forms of the gentle hills that surround it and recalls the character of some nearby aircraft hangars. A combination of good siting and fin walls of board-finished concrete (which repeat the roof's curves) shield the loading dock and maintenance areas from most views and further relate the building to the land. An entrance canopy of transparent plexiglass on an aluminum frame adds a welcome light touch; it is held away from the room surface by a constant dimension, necessitating an intriguing compound curve where the two elements almost meet.

But there are some interruptions to that otherwise inviolable roof: 10 futuristic aluminum-sheathed snouts. Exotic enough by day, at night they begin to glow with a fiery red light, suggesting infernal mysteries beneath the roof. While not quite infernal, the spaces within the building are far from bland, partly due to the effects of those snouts, which are, of course, skylights into the building's central U-shaped corridor, their red glow coming from rings of red neon within them. Both night and day (the building must operate around the clock) these devices add either warm color or occasional patches of direct sunlight to the windowless interior. They also contribute to a system of color coding that provides some sense of orientation despite the lack of outside views: The skylighted corridor is coded red, the central computer room it wraps around is blue, and auxiliary offices and equipment rooms around the perimeter of the building are green. A further refinement to the coding is that, in the perimeter rooms, exterior walls are deep green, interior partitions light green. Aluminum strip ceilings recall the exterior appearance of the building, and the ceiling of the computer room has been vaulted to repeat the exterior form and to give suitable architectural significance to the functional heart of the building.

ROCC is not a building of exquisite detailing. How could it be? But in the jumble of its context it has an authoritative presence, and it provides a working environment that is genuinely civilized. Stetson/Dale has accomplished an exemplary triumph of design over design restrictions. ☐

Above, looking up into one of the skylights, enlivened by rings of red neon. Right, the skylighted corridor. Building plan on wall aids orientation in the windowless building, explains color coding of building areas. Across page, two views of the display room at the heart of the building. Vaulted ceiling is of aluminum slats; walls are covered with acoustic panels.

An Addition of Space, Light— And Life

I. M. Pei & Partners' west wing of the Boston Museum of Fine Arts. By D.C.

The Boston Museum of Fine Arts was built in 1907 to the design of Guy Lowell and has been growing ever since to the point where in the mid-1970s it contained nearly a half million square feet of space. At that point the private institution commissioned I. M. Pei & Partners to install badly needed temperature and humidity controls to protect its collection, to remodel some of the galleries, and to add another 75,000 square feet to house the new mechanical equipment—and to provide some kinds of spaces that the museum, for all of its size, did not have: attractive places to eat and shop, a suitable auditorium, flexible accommodations for the ever more popular "supershows," the giant touring exhibitions on such subjects as King Tut and Alexander the Great.

Pei organized these facilities in a new west wing, a nice bit of balance in his portfolio to the famous east wing of the National Gallery of Art. The Boston wing, of course, has nowhere near the size, prominence or presence as its Washington near-namesake. But the two do have one thing in common: They are each organized around a large skylit space. In Washington it is a voluminous, triangular central court. In Boston it is a vaulted galleria 200 feet long with a canopy of tinted glass and aluminum screening.

There are two levels of circulation along the galleria. On the first it is flanked by the large bookstore on one side and the 380-seat auditorium on the other. Beneath large trees in planters are the tables of a "sidewalk cafe." On the second level (right) the galleria runs beside the new Graham Gund exhibition hall, and across a gulf of space is a new restaurant.

On both levels the galleria is a light-filled, lively place. It speaks clearly to the point of the new west wing being the outgoing, welcoming part of the museum, the most public part—and of the new importance of public use and support to museums everywhere. They can no longer be hushed, cloistered, curatorial places and survive.

The galleria does more than visually and physically link the new spaces in the west wing. It encloses a court that brings still more light to the restaurant, the bookstore and a downstairs

Steve Rosenthal

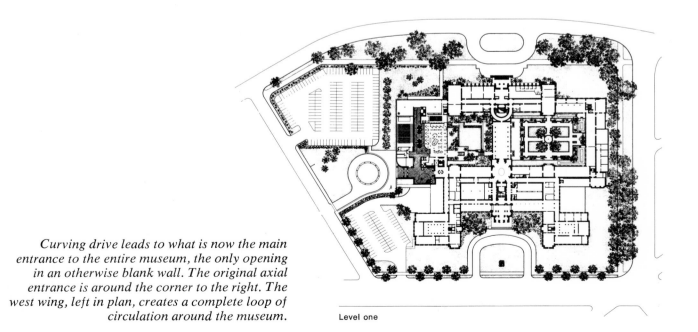

Curving drive leads to what is now the main entrance to the entire museum, the only opening in an otherwise blank wall. The original axial entrance is around the corner to the right. The west wing, left in plan, creates a complete loop of circulation around the museum.

Level one

Completing a loop and creating a new entrance.

cafeteria. And it completes a circulation loop for the entire museum, whose major wings previously were dead-ended. The bright new spaces of the west wing come in a very plain wrapper. Exterior walls are of the same Deer Isle granite as the original, but emphatically without the original's classical elaboration. The long west wall facing the parking lot is completely blank except for a single sharply cut opening at the south corner. This opening, with a lone dark column and concrete lintel, is now the main entrance for the entire museum.

The former front entrance, on the south facade, proudly proclaimed itself with a brace of ionic columns rising to a pediment and acroteria. The new entrance is announced by a void. It has a certain minimalist drama but it raises considerable questions of suitability and compatibility.

The wall curves inward at the entrance, leading to a concrete lobby with an arc cut from its ceiling around an escalator to the second level of the galleria. At this point the visitor can go up, go left to the galleria's lower level or proceed straight ahead into the main portions of the museum.

This entry point to the museum, and the other doors between it and the west wing, can be closed to allow the west wing to operate independently when the rest is shut down. There is a regular schedule of concerts and other evening events here, and some of the big exhibitions remain open after the main museum closes.

The west wing thus has a very lively life of its own and has become one of Boston's leading cultural "draws." It also has an almost festive, highly sophisticated atmosphere of its own. This is most dramatically expressed where the bookstore and restaurant meet the galleria. They do so in a curving, slightly tinted, two-story wall of glass punctuated by projecting glass mullions. Outside the wall is a row of two-story columns bearing bands of mirrors. Along the galleria is a row of bare lights behind glass discs, their glitter caught in the mirrors and the glass walls. The place sparkles. It would have made a good setting for an early Fred Astaire movie.

The large new Gund gallery, by contrast, is a subdued place. The ceiling is made of 15-foot-square coffers whose edges are grooved to receive partitions, so that the gallery can function as one huge space or many small ones with variations in between. Admittance of light is carefully controlled. Each coffer is topped by a combination natural and artificial light fixture: a five-foot-square skylight of partly clear and partly opaque acrylic, containing fluorescent and incandescent lamps, with a prismatic lens. The skylights can be dimmed or closed off entirely by means of fabric screens.

For all of its plainness outside, the west wing is a virtuoso performance in the use of those most basic architectural elements, space and light. □

73

Left, the lower level of the galleria with its tree-shaded 'sidewalk cafe.' At right, the entry, with a swirling opening admitting light from the galleria's aluminum and glass canopy high overhead, inviting ascent (below).

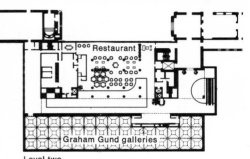

Level two

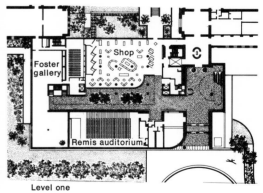

Level one

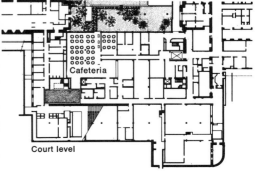

Court level

75

Photographs by Steve Rosenthal

Above, one of the new gallery spaces created at the north end of the galleria at both levels. Below, one of the Gund gallery's versatile coffers, which add volume and provide very controllable light, natural and artificial. Across page, the glittering glass wall of the bookstore and a mirrored column.

76

Streamlined Shapes Enclose a Splendid

Workplace

CRS' Herman Miller Seating Plant in Holland, Mich. By A.O.D.

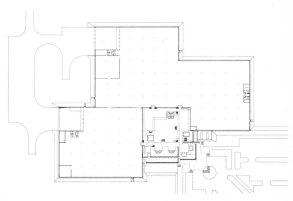

So streamlined and sleek that it could be in motion, the building looks more firmly grounded at its entrance elevation (above), with its contrasting colors and materials, than at its rear (left), which appears as a continuous slick, stainless metal extrusion.

Photographs by Balthazar Korab

Photographs by Balthazar Korab

This building is a benchmark in the history of Herman Miller: The ur-modernist furniture designer and manufacturer has abandoned for the moment its lower-case-helvetica-flush-left image for a more relaxed, tolerant and cheerful approach. Yet its underlying concerns remain consistent with Bauhaus modernism. These consist of an almost missionary belief that thoughtful and distinguished design does contribute to improved working and living conditions.

The Bauhaus, of course, derived its idealism from early 20th century European socialism, while Herman Miller's grew out of the American labor movement and is rooted in principles developed by Joseph Scanlon—a sometime production worker, boxer, cost accountant, college professor and union leader. Beginning during the Depression Scanlon helped economically beleaguered corporations survive by replacing their typical adversarial approach toward labor with a democratic one stressing management and workers' shared interests. Herman Miller's president, Max De Pree, became a convert in 1950 after attending one of Scanlon's lectures in Grand Rapids.

"Scanlon," as Herman Miller employees call it, is an attitude rather than a plan or method. It assumes that people want to work, want responsibility and need to feel both a sense of accomplishment and of belonging to a productive work group. It also assumes employees deserve competent management and certain rights. A tangible consequence of "Scanlon" is that Herman Miller employees share in the company's ownership and have virtual job security after two years' employment.

To an outsider listening to Millerites debate whether something is "good" or "bad Scanlon," the argument can sound quasi-theological. It is clear, though, that they take such discussion seriously, mean it when they say "Scanlon" plays a decisive role in determining the look and feel of a Herman Miller building, and

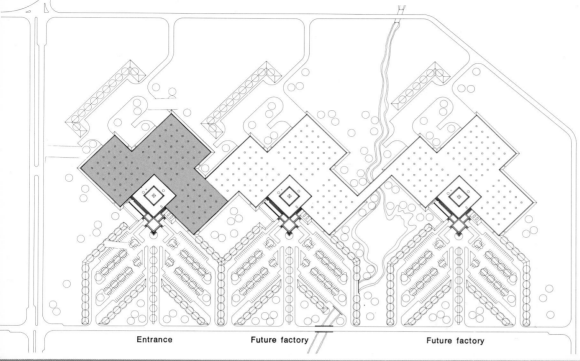

Entrance Future factory Future factory

What is now the entrance
courtyard (below) will,
when funds become avail-
able, be turned into a 'people place' with a cafeteria
and central glass-covered
lounge. One of the build-
ing's intriguing details
(across page, above) is a
slanted slice of glazing, right
of the entrance. The master
plan (left) calls for two additional, interconnected
buildings identical to the
existing one.

The interior is colorful, cheerful and seems of manageable size, since its bulk is broken up into a pinwheel. Above, chairs are stored on moveable racks; at right, just off the entryway, are offices for supervisors. A semblance of individual turf is provided by wooden frames between work spaces (across page, above).

Comfortable scale and democratic daylighting.

that the Seating Plant in Holland, Mich., by CRS, with Paul Kennon as design partner, is "good Scanlon." That is, it deals sensitively with social as well as esthetic issues.

Herman Miller has recently been growing at a rate of close to 70 percent a year, which has created congestion and confusion at the Zeeland headquarters. As Tom Wolterinck, vice president of facilities management, explains, "We like to keep our organization of small groups so that we can communicate openly. So we made a decision to create a new plant in commuting distance of the main site." The firm bought 80 acres of farmland adjacent to a small airport being expanded into a full service jetport that will become the "front door of Herman Miller," in Wolterinck's words. The plan is to develop this site as an industrial park with the Holland Seating Plant establishing the overall image.

It is an unexpected image, a futuristic, streamlined, hovering object with a pinwheel-like plan; at night, it looks like a great, glowing spaceship. Because the building is in a flood plain area, CRS surrounded it with a dike, bermed it and lined the first four feet of interior elevation with poured concrete. The structure's standard steel frame and metal panel construction system, tightly wrapped with no sharp edges, looks suspended between

two continuous strips of glazing. Below, a two-foot-high strip of windows angles down to rest on the concrete base; above is an uninterrupted clerestory curved at the top to create a rounded, somewhat indeterminate roofline. Because one of the approaches by car to the Seating Plant is from a high overpass, Kennon attempted to make the roof into a fifth, attractive facade, "so you didn't drive on the overpass, look down and see nothing but junk on the roof," as he puts it. That attempt, he says, was the derivation of the curving clerestory band and of the skylights dotting the roof.

The most important function, however, of all the glazing is its effect on the building's interior. The canted ribbon of operable windows at eye level is for views and ventilation, the wraparound clerestory and skylights for natural light. Because none of the building's walls is longer than 200 feet, no worker is more than 100 feet from a window. Nor are any of the three interconnected petals of the pinwheel plan larger than 80,000 square feet because, Wolterinck says, "we've found that in bigger spaces than that a person starts feeling lost in space."

There is no chance of that happening here. This building of hard concrete, steel and glass is a downright cozy place, not only because of its comfortable scale and airiness, but because of its cheerful colors. Trusses, beams, joists, columns, ducts, pipes are

Axonometric detail shows the wall system of demountable stainless steel panels and curved clerestories over a standard steel frame. At right is a detail of the building at night, aglow, with its insides etched at top and bottom against the light.

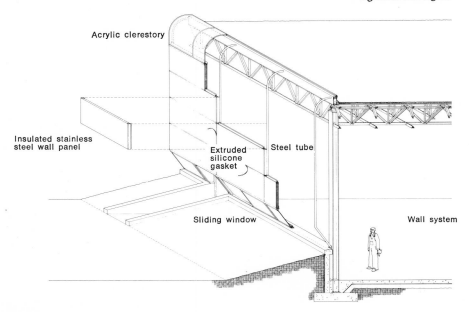

Acrylic clerestory

Insulated stainless steel wall panel

Extruded silicone gasket

Steel tube

Sliding window

Wall system

Making design decisions serve multiple purposes.

all exposed and painted. (Wrapped as it is in a tightly folded, almost seamless envelope and with its use of structural elements as decoration, the Seating Plant bears a decided resemblance to some of Helmuth Jahn's buildings.) Wolterinck is apologetic about the abundant use of color, feeling it's overdone; it is not. Kennon laughs nervously when asked about the sodium vapor lights suspended from the steel deck. But even the lighting is surprisingly unoffensive, mostly because its effect is diluted by plentiful natural light. Sodium vapor was chosen, of course, for its spare use of energy.

The attempt to be energy efficient is yet another reason for the clerestory and the band of operable windows, the building's only cooling device. In fact, most design decisions made for the Seating Plant serve two or more purposes. The dike surrounding the structure not only prevents flooding but acts as an insulating barrier, since it places a significant portion of the building below grade. The metal sandwich panels were selected for energy and cost as well as esthetic reasons. Says Wolterinck, "We figured that using a stainless steel skin, a lot of styrofoam as infill and aluminum interior panels we could get an excellent insulation factor." Moreover, the panels are clipped together and gasketed, so when Herman Miller expands the building—the plan is to add on two more interconnected pinwheels—the panels can be demounted and moved, erector-set fashion. Overall, the building is designed with a quick intelligence that doesn't advertise its cleverness.

One element that Herman Miller and CRS regard as key for the building—and very good "Scanlon"—remains to be built. It will be a skylit, landscaped entrance at the center of the pinwheel, surrounded by offices, containing a cafeteria and serving as a general gathering spot for all workers. Even without this "people place," as they call it, the Seating Plant is already a splendid place for people to work and be. □

84

Balthazar Korab

Whither Architecture? Some Outside Views

In a real sense no one is "outside" of architecture. All of us live in it, with it. The contributors of the following essays are outside only in the sense that they are not in the profession or its schools; they are consumers of architecture rather than producers of it. They were asked two questions: "What do you see as major trends in American architecture? What do you think of them?" We are enormously grateful to them for taking the time to respond, and for responding so thoughtfully. The editors.

Henry Fairlie: 'We do not need architecture to surprise; we need it above all to be familiar, and strengthen our delight in it.'

Even if there can be an art for art's sake—which is doubtful, without it self-destructing—there cannot be an architecture for architecture's sake. "Only your art," Auden bows to the composer, "is pure contraption." The only architecture that I can think of that approaches pure contraption is the original Labyrinth or the Hampton Court maze (plan below). Not only does one get lost in them, they are contrived so that one gets lost.

That is not helpful; not even, after a time, very amusing. But architecture is meant to be helpful. Its purpose is to enable us to get about it, to do whatever we wish or need to do, conveniently and fittingly; and to do it—this is the art—with an added satisfaction, enjoyment or even exhilaration. We cannot do this in an architectural drawing or a book of architectural theory. *Si monumentum requiris, circumspice* would not mean much as Wren's epitaph if, instead of being on the wall of his cathedral, it were on one of his drawings.

These opening observations may be simple, but that is the layman's privilege. I first fell in love with architecture on my family's farms in Scotland. The farm buildings in Scotland are called "the steading." It is a wonderfully strong and telling word. It speaks of buildings rooted in a place and, of course, it is echoed in the more commonplace "homestead."

My main impression of the steading, as a boy, was that it would always remain. Year after year, it would stay. I do not think much of architecture that does not give the feeling of being rooted. I was still quite young at the time of the Festival of Britain in 1951. The best of its buildings —as suited a festival—were fanciful and aëry. They were delightful and, in the drabness of London after the war, lifted our spirits. But it was a calamity when architects, under their influence, tried to duplicate them for everyday buildings. Everyday is not a festival. Everyday is substantial, and its buildings should be.

Buildings should not only serve, but represent and symbolize, the functions for which we use them. Churches should look and feel like churches—and not, as some modern ones do, like drive-ins—and houses should look and feel like houses. No one I know chooses a bank unless its walls at least look thick; even the automatic tellers on a street are rightly constructed to seem like a safe.

But then there is this paradox. Architecture exists to serve a purpose—to be helpful, as I have said—but it is more looked at than any other art. People do not have to go to a gallery to see it or to a concert hall to hear it or a library to read it, for it is all around them from waking to sleeping. It is still there even while they are sleeping. There are modern bedrooms that seem to have been designed for insomniacs. But most of us choose a bedroom in which we close our eyes at night, and wake to in the morning, which is not fussily distracting and above all is private and rather cozy.

People see architecture, then, more than any other art. Yet this does not seem, these days, to satisfy many architects. It does not seem to be enough for them that people cannot help seeing their buildings; they are anxious to draw people's attention to them and force a strong reaction. Too much modern architecture is designed to compel involuntary expressions of surprise. I find this odd since its task is above all to supply the familiar.

Since art moved from the walls where we live into the galleries, it has become

a mistress and scandalously a very fickle one. We can say of modern painting what Stanley Baldwin said of the press lords in Britain: that it claims power without responsibility, which has been the prerogative of the harlot throughout the ages." We must go to visit art—she is not at our home—and take her presents. We must applaud her; she must entertain. She is too, too divine; and she, in return, must surprise. But she never cooks. The relationship has its excitements for a time. I do not deny that. But we are married to architecture.

We do not need architecture to surprise; we need it above all to be familiar, and strengthen our delight in it. This does not mean that a good architect will not surprise us now and then with something unexpected. But then so does a good wife (or husband), usually more entertainingly than a mistress (or lover). The point is this: It does not really matter if we cannot find a painting, whereas it often does matter if we cannot find a building.

One used to be able to spot any bank in England because it was built in what Osbert Lancaster called "Bankers' Georgian." I find it helpful in America that most post offices from coast to coast look very much like each other and can be spotted even in a strange block in a strange city.

Modern (by which I also mean postmodern) architecture—I cannot here play with the labels and jargon—seems to me to have been more successful than any other art. (That may not be saying very much.) The reason is that, however much it struggles to escape, it is tied to the everyday. Mary McCarthy once said that the novel needed to return from the pole of myth to the pole of journalism. The novel ought to deal with the quotidian, as it did in the hands of Dickens or Balzac. Architecture is bound to deal with the quotidian. Every fault in modern architecture springs from its unwillingness to obey its worldly duties.

All art has to cultivate obedience to something that is other than itself. Otherwise it loses its way. Architecture is fortunate that, more than any other art, it *must* obey those who need its buildings. Yet too many architects seem to regard this as subservience. This is like a journalist who thinks that he cannot be a good writer if he puts first his readers' wish to have the news.

Let me end with two stories as parables. When I worked on *The Times* of London after the war, I used to visit at lunchtime the Wren churches in the city, as they were being rebuilt after the Blitz. It was like walking through a primer of architecture. The elder friend who was my guide pointed to the famous oval dome in one of them with its apparently supporting columns. But they are not supporting the dome. Wren had designed a dome that needed no columns. The guild that had ordered the church believed in his experiment no more than we would trust a plane without wings. Did Wren throw an artist's tantrum? No! He put in the columns to reassure his patrons—but with an inch between each of them and the dome. All art today, but especially architecture, needs that humility.

The second story is told by George Seferis. He showed a friend a painting of a baker's shop where the trays that carried the loaves from the ovens were held at such an angle that the friend said that the loaves would fall off the trays in real life. Seferis let the artist reply: "Ah! In real life, maybe. But in my painting the loaves don't fall off." That is art's license. But the architect does not have that license. He must build a bakery where bakers can work well, with floors that are even and trays that don't slope. There is a world of difference between Wren's dome, which he knew would hold itself up, and the artist's tray from which the loaves would fall.

It is precisely this challenge that makes architecture by far the most important of the arts—it must work for us—and it is precisely the dissatisfaction with this that has led so much architecture into realms of pure contraption. Today's "movements" in architecture seem to me, at their best, to be efforts to return from pure contraption to the ground of everyday.

J. Irwin Miller: 'I would hope that architects might rediscover the meaning of their own word, which is chief builder.'

The startling innovations of American high technology appear to have stimulated, but also to have infected, our current architectural practice.

Innovation and innovators are now praised by architectural critics, and innovation for itself is feverishly pursued by much of the profession. In the world of art, it is worth noting that the innovator has not always been the giant among peers. Bach did not write the first fugue, nor Shakespeare the first sonnet.

I imagine that today's architect has now at his hand more than enough materials, techniques and tools for the achievement of lasting greatness. That greatness, if it comes, will proceed not so much from innovation, or from being different for the sake of being different, as it will from maturity, from intellect and from unselfconscious commitment to do one's best, abhoring fashion and fad.

The best of tomorrow's architects will

not look over their shoulders at critics or at anyone, but will rather be their own sternest judges. I would hope that the present degree of frivolity in American architecture might disappear, and that innovation would begin to be valued only when it offered a better way.

Finally, I would hope that architects might rediscover the meaning of their own word, which is "chief builder," and that they would move away from the limited role they too often assign themselves today, that of "chief designer," and once more, and in new terms, shoulder the comprehensive responsibility of "chief builder." This I take to be the simultaneous satisfaction of the client's true needs, large and small, and the realization of the architect's highest potential.

John B. Jackson: 'The layman does not accept modernism because it is beautiful, but because he finds that it works.'

Americans have had more than 50 years in which to get used to what we call the modern style in architecture. At first it bothered and sometimes shocked us, but that was long ago. We have learned to accept it as part of our workaday world and even to associate it with certain contemporary values. The school we go to, the office or plant where we work, the museum, the library, the shopping center we visit, even the hospital where we were born, are probably all examples—good or bad—of the modern style.

It is true that familiarity in itself does not necessarily mean that we have any real understanding of the modern esthetic canon, but in the long run I think it produces a sense of what to look for in the way of forms and spaces and surfaces and relationships, and above all it produces expectations of a special kind of environment. The layman does not accept mod-

Henry Fairlie, British-born journalist living in Washington, D.C., writes a column for the *Washington Post* and contributes to such magazines as *Harper's, New Republic* and *National Review.*
J. Irwin Miller is chairman of Cummins Engine Co. in Columbus, Ind. In 1954, as head of the Cummins Foundation, he started the architectural program that has resulted in more than 40 buildings in the Columbus area designed by first-rank architects. **John B. Jackson,** landscape architect and educator, is author of *The Southern Landscape Tradition* and *American Space: The Centennial Years.* He lives near Santa Fe, N.M.

ernism because he finds it beautiful, but because he finds that it works, and so he is sometimes more sensitive to change than the architect is.

Writing as a layman who has watched the style evolve in the smaller cities of America over half a century, let me suggest a few of the ways in that it seems to have matured and come of age.

The most conspicuous change that I have noticed is in the relationship between architecture and the urban plan. We have always thought of them as inseparable. The Renaissance, perhaps because of the importance it attached to the facades of buildings, did much to make urban architecture a decorative feature of the street. The row upon row of similar facades contributed to the glorification of the Baroque *Prunkstrasse* or representational avenue. One of the basic objectives of modernism in its early days was to free architecture from this subordinate role.

Le Corbusier surrounded his highrise buildings with green parks and sited them far from the street. But it remained for a later generation, especially here in America, to see that motorized traffic was destroying streetside architecture, and to establish a new and more balanced relationship between building and street. We eventually, and largely by accident, gave the building its independence and allowed it to join with other buildings to form a self-contained complex with its own surrounding spaces, its own orientation, its own patterns of movement. Withdrawn at a safe distance from the rapid, all but uninterrupted flow of traffic, these complexes assume many new forms: office complexes, shopping complexes, sports and convention complexes. Small specialty shops, the first victims of the motorized street, become boutiques and take refuge in back alleys and converted warehouses.

So now the modern building has its protective buffer zone of drive-in facilities, parking lots and carefully landscaped open spaces or plazas. A prestigious business address is no longer (say) "111 Lincoln Street," it is "American Insurance Square" or "First National Plaza." Texas modernism seems to favor "tower" as a desirable address, but the principle is the same: The building is liberated from the tyranny of the street and begins to emerge as an autonomous environment.

By this I mean that the modern building—school or office highrise or shopping center or whatever—is rapidly evolving as the container of a self-sufficient, manmade environment. I would say that the first step in this redefining of the building was the wholesale installation, in the 1950s, of airconditioning in places of work. It was soon followed by sophisticated lighting systems designed to produce not only better lighting but to differentiate various kinds of space and to foster moods of one sort or another. Both airconditioning and new lighting enlarged work areas and changed office and factory layouts.

Sensory response to the building as a self-contained environment was further enriched by the introduction of acoustical walls and ceilings and piped-in music. Perhaps we should include wall-to-wall carpeting as still another environmental improvement. But who can enumerate the many devices meant to establish the environmental self-sufficiency of the contemporary consumer-oriented building— shopping center, hotel, hospital or office? The resplendent tropical landscaping— replaced every six weeks—in lobbies and malls and waiting rooms, the carefully engineered color codes, the reassuring textures of walls and upholstery, the artful shifts in floor levels and ceiling heights? Not one of these innovations, it is safe to say, was ever dreamt of by the early masters of the modern style, but they are now essential. What is more, they are all justified by developers and promoters and designers as expressions of unimpeachably progressive ideas: energy conservation, efficiency, health and safety, and the dignity of the common man.

A third change has been this: Modernism has become the idiom of the public sector; it is more and more identified with buildings intended to serve a very heterogeneous public. Those who lived in the years when modernism (or as we called it then, the International Style) was introduced to this country will remember how little it was noticed outside of a small group of art and architecture critics, how it was appraised almost entirely in esthetic terms and how strongly its democratization was resisted. I am inclined to think we overlook the popularization and commercialization of what we now call art deco as a factor in the public acceptance of modernism. Art deco was never a true style, it was an attempt to soften and "humanize" the radical new forms of the modern style. By and large it succeeded.

'Resplendant tropical landscaping': The Ford Foundation by Roche Dinkeloo.

It replaced traditional styles—burdened as they were with history and class distinctions and symbolism—by a style which was novel and ingratiating, easy to understand and adapt, with an essentially meaningless ornamentation, useful in all large, impersonal spaces.

This was the influence that changed modernism in America and made it what it now is: the appropriate style for buildings used by a wide public. This was the influence that in the eyes of the more severe critics destroyed the purity of true modernism and led to its downfall. But critics overlook the difference between the way the bureaucracy, the establishment, handled the public in the past—and still does in much of the Old World—and how we try to handle the public in America. By law as well as by general consensus the American public means *everyone* regardless of class or age or physical condition or degree of schooling, and for such a public we have sought to devise an architecture accessible to all.

We have paid a high price, esthetically speaking. We have been obliged to eliminate all subtleties and refinements in design, all experimentation and surprise in favor of easily interpreted forms and space; we have eliminated all solemnity and disturbing symbolism in favor of friendly, easily understood signs and topical references. Exteriors and interiors in the modern public oriented building abound in what are called redundant clues: Messages that are both visible and audible and even bodily designed to inform and protect and reassure the public. Our buildings aspire to be accident proof, fireproof, vandal proof and foolproof. We are less concerned with art than with with producing a man-made environment that contributes to the physical and psychological well being of every man, woman and child who enters.

Are we succeeding? Not altogether, but give us time. I think there are innumerable changes of this pragmatic sort waiting for us in the years ahead. We need not expect them to produce a new style in the sense of new forms, but perhaps we are the victims of a faulty reading of recent architectural history. The modernism that we see being built in contemporary America, and that the architectural critic easily dismisses as without significance, does not derive from the principles enunciated in the first decades of this century. It derives from the discovery or invention of the building as a planned, self-contained environment. The first phase of modernism was the structural-mechanical phase, and it lasted until the 1950s. The second phase, the phase we are in, is the biological-environmental phase. The third, when it comes, will be the phase that discovers the religious ingredient in our efforts to build better houses and a better world.

Ezra Stoller © ESTO

Norman Cousins: 'Architecture is the one art where standing on the shoulders of one's predecessors can be done without apology.'

Architecture as an art is unique in that the materials it employs make possible new advances and departures. True, other art forms benefit from invention or innovation. New musical instruments that came into being over the centuries gave enlarged capabilities to collective endeavor, culminating in the symphony orchestra, just as new discoveries and refinements have widened the capacities of the sculptor or artist. But architecture, of all the arts, has the highest ability to transcend itself and create new art forms through materials made available to it by science and technology. The skyscraper was made possible by structural steel. Reinforced concrete opened up other departures. Aluminum and glass led to broad new trends in design. And now, new lightweight materials, in combination with existing ones, will set the stage for architectural artistry on a scale that compares favorably with other great advances of the 20th century.

My hope is that the new thrust will not lose itself in playing games with secondary forms, such as ornamental and interacting cubes, triangles and semicircles, even though these ancient devices may provide welcome relief from the overused boxes and straight lines. There are indigenous possibilities that can be opened up by the wide array of new materials (as well as computer aids for full utilization) —possibilities that can lead to strong evolutionary development. It is not necessary to concoct revolutionary designs. The main need now, as always, is to build on tradition. Architecture is the one art where standing on the shoulders of one's predecessors can be done without apology or self-consciousness or diminution of distinction.

In terms of current American achievement, I would hope that more attention will be given to the kind of projects being undertaken in cities like Tulsa. The spotlight has been on the redevelopment projects in major cities like Pittsburgh, Detroit, Houston and Philadelphia. Important undertakings in smaller centers

Norman Cousins edited *The Saturday Review of Literature* from 1940-71 and from 1973-77. He currently chairs the magazine's editorial board and is a senior lecturer at the University of California at Los Angeles. **Wilcomb E. Washburn,** a historian, directs the Smithsonian Institution's office of American studies.

tend to be minimized or overlooked. To my mind, the rebuilding of downtown Tulsa being carried out by the Williams brothers is civically as significant and esthetically satisfying as anything being undertaken in the larger metropolitan centers. What is especially appealing about the Tulsa development is that function and artistry are being beautifully blended. The historic buildings are being maintained and refurbished. The new buildings derive their appeal not just from their intrinsic design but by their relationship to surrounding space and structure. The cultural center is not segregated but is an integral part of the new area, which includes business, municipal, federal and state facilities.

In general, the heartland of America provides encouraging evidence that architecture is a powerful foundation for the rational and creative life of a community.

Wilcomb E. Washburn: 'Urban form is no longer sensed as something in contrast to nature or imposed upon nature but as nature itself.'

The most significant trend in architecture today is the integration of urban and landscape design. Traditionally these concerns have been at opposite ends of the design spectrum. Today they are moving together. Why? Because the urban form is no longer sensed as something in contrast to nature or imposed upon nature but as nature itself, or a legitimate substitute for nature. This is not to say that the trend is evident and apparent to all architects. It is not; indeed, it is probably barely recognized by most. But it is a trend nevertheless since it is based on the imperatives of nature and will thereby ineluctably emerge in the formal esthetics of architecture.

Ian L. McHarg in his 1969 book, *Design With Nature,* cited Washington, D.C., as an example of an urban development sensitively related to the nature in which it was lovingly placed by Pierre Charles L'Enfant and his successors. McHarg showed how Washington was built into the geology of the area and utilized the tidal flats, the escarpment surrounding the base of the "bowl," and the summits, ridges and rivers to which the avenues and public buildings of the federal city are related. "The image of Washington," as he put it, "is of a great city meeting a great river." The city, McHarg noted, has a distinct "landscape identity."

What has happened in Washington, as elsewhere, in the last 10 years, is that the

advance of technology and burgeoning population can no longer be comfortably accommodated within the landscape identity defined for Washington, and for most other cities in the world, in earlier centuries. Today's architect is faced with a new challenge to relate his work to the pre-existing landscape identity of the city within which he is building urban elements, or to redefine that identity. Too often in the past the architect has ignored the context, sometimes deliberately in order to make a "flagship" building that will stand out from its neighbors and dominate the landscape.

The principal distinguishing feature of the "landscape identity" of the evolving world city is its verticality. Technology, land values and population increases have combined to make the most distinctive feature of urban growth its shaping of vertical space rather than its horizontal extension. A book that focuses upon this vertical emphasis is Wayne Attoe's *Skylines: Understanding and Molding Urban Silhouettes* (New York: John Wiley, 1981). The shape or nature of the skyline, Attoe points out, "has figured little in urban and social planning" because other factors— employment, quality of housing, crime rate, income, schools, climate, etc. seem more important in people's lives. Yet the skyline will become of increasing importance in the future as the effects of insensitive and unregulated building take place.

There is now unmistakable evidence of the erosion of the green edge of the topographic bowl surrounding the federal city. Despite the ability of planning agencies in the federal city to control growth in the District of Columbia, the massive and anticontextual character of the construction in the Rosslyn, Va., area just across the Potomac from Washington has begun to shut off one of the gateways through the natural edge of the topographic bowl, and to create a menacing intrusion into the visual environment of the monumental area. The buildings in the Rosslyn area are generally cash-register and computer-design type containers of rentable office space lacking any relationship to the sacred precincts they abut. Yet they could have been designed individually and as a group to provide the 20th century equivalent of the visual punctuation points that L'Enfant's fountains and statues sought to achieve in the periodic squares and circles he designed along Washington's main avenues. The modern urban architect must meet the challenge of accommodating 20th century mass construction to cityscapes often incorporating 18th century delicacy and 19th century grace.

The experience of San Francisco is perhaps the best object lesson of why architects and developers will in the future be required to be more sensitive to the

continued on page 128

AIA Honor Awards 1982

This year the American Institute of Architects honored 12 new and extended use projects in its annual tribute to design excellence.

The eight new buildings chosen "are sensitive to and fit easily into their surroundings, avoiding harsh juxtapositions of scale and treatment," said current use jury chairwoman Joan E. Goody, AIA. "Spatial organization is conceived for the benefit of the user, rather than to satisfy a preconceived geometric order. Appropriate use of traditional building materials and methods has produced a variety of solutions with appealing textures and colors." The jury noted the preponderance of modest and low-tech commissions in the "final pool" of projects. "We had anticipated more examples of design that could represent solutions to the many large scale, socially significant or technologically difficult building problems facing us today," Goody said.

The buildings honored include the new headquarters of the American Academy of Arts and Sciences in Cambridge, Mass. (page 16); three energy-efficient houses—one in East Hampton, N.Y., one in the West Indies and the other on a lake near Minneapolis; two projects located on steep hills in San Francisco —an elementary school and condominium complex; a library for the blind and handicapped in an inner-city neighborhood in Chicago, and a pavilion in downtown Phoenix (right).

Other jury members for new work were Howard Barnstone, FAIA; Thomas Beeby, AIA; Gary Chan, a student at the University of Washington; John O. Merrill Jr., FAIA; Jay C. McAmis, associate AIA member, and Robert Venturi, FAIA.

The jury for extended use felt "that while the quality of restoration in the United States had markedly improved in the recent years, the quality of work that demands an interviewing of old and new still generally falls short of the quality of the best new design," said chairman Frank O. Gehry, FAIA. The jury chose three projects recognized for "sensitive, knowledgeable and technically proficient restoration." They include the renovations of a Prairie School commercial building, an art deco bank and 43 houses in a Victorian neighborhood. Only one building, a residence in Princeton, N.J., was chosen for combining the old with the new.

The other jurors included Bruce A. Abrahamson, FAIA; Dora P. Crouch, associate professor of architectural history, Rensselaer Polytechnic Institute; Mark Lowe Fisher, associate AIA member; Pamela Jenkins, student, Pratt Institute; Nory Miller, senior editor, *Progressive Architecture,* and Peter Papademetriou, AIA. *Nora Richter Greer*

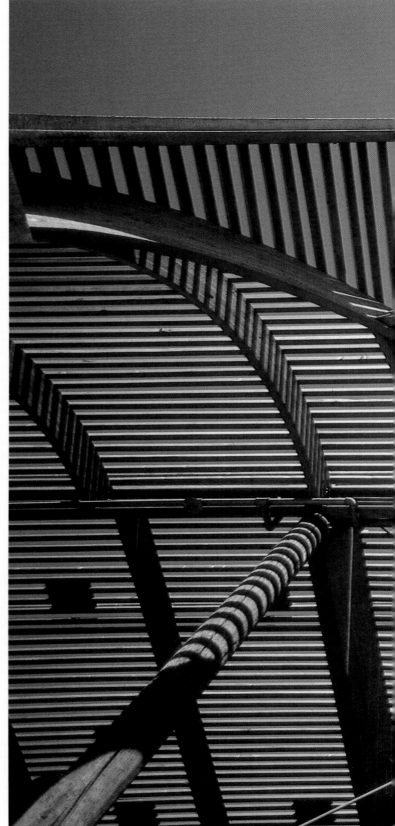

Wayne Thom Associates

Lath Pavilion for a Downtown Park

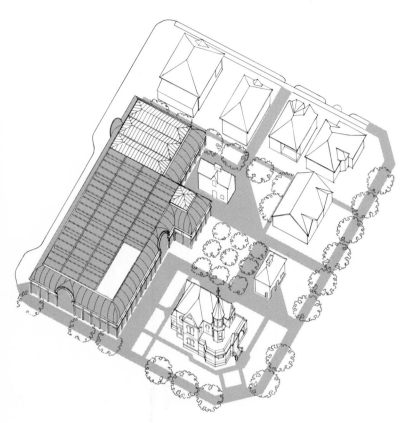

Located in the heart of Phoenix are the final remnants of the city's original site—the Rosson House and surrounding barns, bungalows and gardens. Restored as a community activity center, the structures proved too small to accommodate large crowds, so an outdoor pavilion, the Lath House, was added.

The pavilion is made of pressure-treated 2x3-inch wood lath supported by glue-laminated beams and curved purlins. Beneath the lath umbrella is a stuccoed wood frame building containing meeting rooms, catering kitchen, public toilets and the caretaker's apartment. The 22,800-square-foot pavilion and frame building can hold as many as 1,000 persons for such events as sit-down dinners, fashion shows and concerts. Eventually, a greenhouse will be added. The pavilion is designed to provide welcome shade on hot summer days but be transparent enough for views of the surrounding buildings that are listed on the National Register of Historic Places (Rosson House as seen from the Lath House, right).

The jury commended the architect, Robert R. Frankeberger, AIA, Phoenix, for the "great skill" that is "evidenced in this handcrafted pavilion's sizing, proportion and sensitive interplay of wood textures, and light and shadow."

Client: Rosson House/Heritage Square Foundation, John Diggs, president, for the City of Phoenix. Structural engineer: Caruso Engineering Associates, Inc. Mechanical and electrical engineers: Lowry-Sorenson-Willcoxson Engineers. Landscape architect: Jim Wheat. General contractors: J. R. Porter Construction Co., Inc. Completed in 1980.

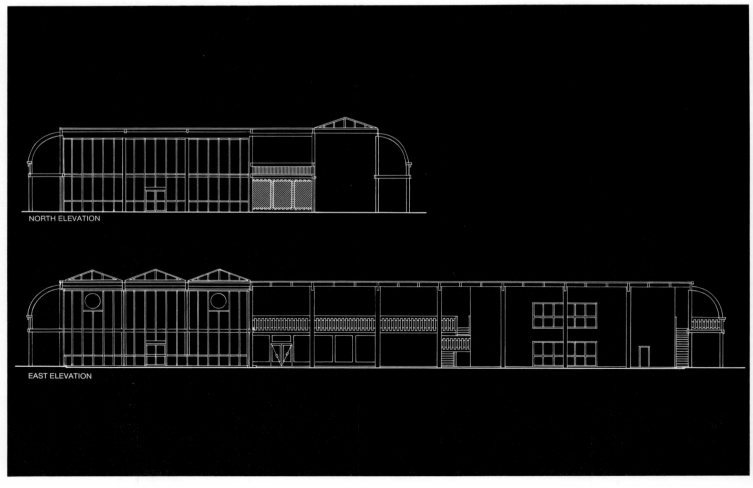

NORTH ELEVATION

EAST ELEVATION

Elementary School Gently Climbs Up Telegraph Hill

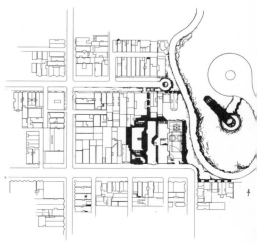

On San Francisco's Telegraph Hill near Coit Tower a small elementary school sits happily among the surrounding residential buildings. It is so successful in hiding its true identity that on first look one could easily mistake it for a small apartment building, if it were not for the sound and sight of children going to school or children's drawings in the window.

The key to its unobtrusiveness is its massing, which emulates the neighboring buildings. Designed by Esherick Homsey Dodge & Davis, San Francisco (George Homsey, principal-in-charge; Barry Baker, project architect), the school is meant to reflect the predominant character of the neighborhood (three-story walkup townhouses) in its street facade. The four-story school steps up the hill (photo left), which, among other things, seems to diminish its 40,000-square-foot size. From the street, the school is seen as three separate modules, each with its own entrance, flanked by courtyards above and below.

This lateral organization reverses the plan of an earlier school on the site that was condemned as seismically unsafe and economically unfeasible to rebuild. (The new school was designed stringently for seismic safety.) The former school's plan placed the major and only playground next to the existing town houses. In the new school the building is separated only partially from its neighbors by the small forecourt, and thus the row of buildings is extended up the hill. By placing the major playground (photo above) at the far side of the school against Coit Tower park, the noise of children playing travels into the park more readily than through the rest of the neighborhood.

The stepped arrangement also allows for magnificent views of the city below and allows the building to take full advantage of San Francisco's mild climate. Internal circulation is kept to a minimum, and exterior passages and promenades, large operable windows and open-air stairways are emphasized. These

Simple, but not quite unadorned.

things combined reduce the need for artificial heating, cooling and lighting throughout the building. (Solar collectors installed on the roof provide domestic hot water.)

Off the lower court are the two kindergarten rooms and behind them the multipurpose room that doubles as a community center. It has its own entrance via a back alley. The second floor houses four classrooms, a special classroom, storage area and administrative offices. All of the building's classrooms are semi-open in plan, each having visual access to a shared kitchen, demonstration and teacher preparation area. On the third floor are six more classrooms, two special classrooms and a media center/library. The library opens onto a terrace greenhouse and outdoor area for the students where the plant world is presented in

a "distinctly urban manner," in the architect's words. The third floor is also connected to the upper play yard. The fourth floor contains four more classrooms. The school can accommodate up to 460 students.

The exterior draws on motifs of the original school, such as the rusticated portal on the front facade, and other schools in San Francisco. And while its stucco exterior and wood frame are boldly colored in orange and ochre, the building's intimate scale and courtyard, exterior passages and simplicity make it a peaceful, inviting building.

Client: San Francisco Unified School District. Structural engineer: Rutherford & Chekene. Mechanical and electrical engineer: Marion Cerbatos Tomasi, Inc. Landscape architect: Richard Schadt Associates, Inc. General contractor: Nibbi Brothers. Completed in 1980.

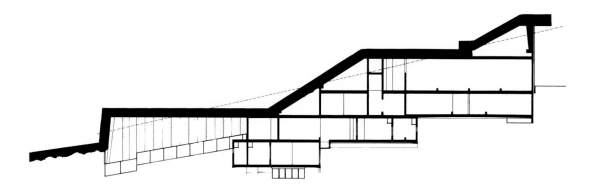

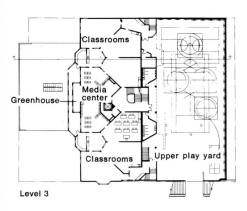

Level 3

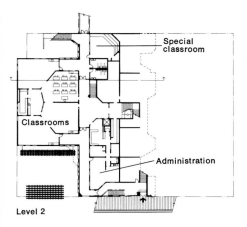

Level 2

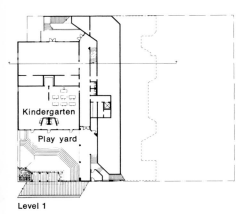

Level 1

From the street the school is seen as three separate modules, left. Exterior passages are used extensively, above right, and classrooms are semiopen, right.

2529

Before exterior renovation, below; and after, left.

Building 'New Pride' While Rebuilding a Neighborhood

Revitalization of an inner-city neighborhood in Denver without displacing its low-income homeowners was the major emphasis behind the Curtis Park Face Block Project. It involved the exterior restoration of 43 houses and neighborhood landscaping, with an average budget of $10,000 per house.

Built in the late 19th century, the neighborhood consists of large houses intermixed with small cottages. In recent years the area suffered serious neglect, and four years ago when the project was initiated many houses were vacant. Although of a mixed population, the district is predominantly Hispanic.

For each residence, a priority list of exterior rehabilitation work was developed by the architect in agreement with the owner. All 43 houses are of brick bearing wall construction with some stone trim. Porches, decks, windows, doors and trim are wood.

The project included exterior renovation of 43 houses. Owners were consulted for all repairs and color schemes. Besides repairing surfaces, improvements included repair of trim, landscaping and fences.

Private efforts spurred by public.

Improvements made included repairing sidewalks, landscaping and fencing; repairing, repointing and cleaning brickwork; repairing or replacing built-up, shingle and roll roofing and flashing, gutters and downspouts; repairing existing trim; reglazing or repairing existing wood doors and windows; installing new wood doors and windows; exterior painting and finishing, and exterior electrical work. Three complete elevation color studies were made for each house, with the owner choosing the exact color scheme. All improvements were in keeping with the Victorian style of the neighborhood. Since seven prime contractors were involved, the improvements on each house were bid separately. (In a parallel program administered by the city agency, funding for all "essential" interior repair and rehabilitation was available.)

The result of the program was a "new pride" in the neighborhood. "Homeowners assisting in the project have a new respect for their community," the architects maintain. And, in turn, more prosperous homeowners in the area have begun renovations with attention to the Victorian details and colors.

The project was funded by HUD, the Department of the Interior, the National Trust for Historic Preservation, the Ampter Foundation, Historic Denver, Inc., Mountain Bell Telephone Co. and the Colorado Division of Housing. The architects involved were Long Hoeft and McCrystal Design, both of Denver.

The jury called the project "a constructive idea recognizing the neighborhood as a viable social entity whose identity can be enhanced through the physical environment." The jury felt that "extensive cohesion had been achieved in the neighborhood. . . . The project was a demonstration of architectural practice in a true service capacity, an important type of professional activity. This allowed present owners to remain in their environment, as well as to see its improvement through the thoughtful attention of the architects involved."

Coordinator: Historic Denver Inc. Structural engineer: KKBNA Consulting Engineers Inc. General contractors: Carrillo Construction Co., Randall Construction Co., Freiboth Construction Co., Yamamoto Construction Co., Garner Construction Co., Arcwight & Hutcher Construction Co. Completed in 1981.

Serious Purpose Adorned By Color

An early example of Stanley Tigerman's "architecture couched in humor, architecture that is fun" (in Tigerman's words) is the Illinois Regional Library for the Blind and Physically Handicapped, Chicago. Completed in 1977, the design combines the playfulness of curved lines, bright colors and illusionary tricks with serious attention to the needs of the users.

The building sits on a small triangular site on Chicago's near west side. The building edges two sides of the triangle; on the third side is the parking lot. The library's use is three-fold: the State of Illinois' distribution center for books and cassettes for the handicapped and Chicago's public library for the blind and

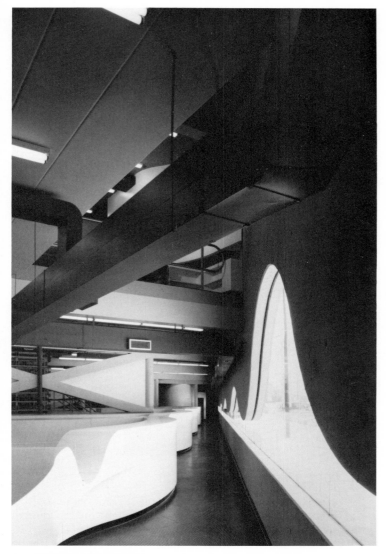

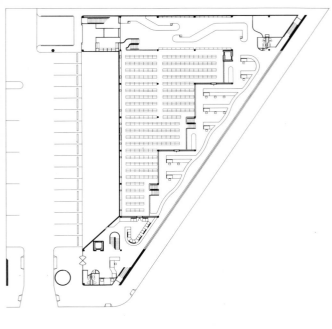

The concrete facade with its curvy window is in contrast with the baked enamel surfaces on the other two sides, below and facing page. The circulation counter repeats the window's shape, left, and spans one side of the first floor.

handicapped are located on the first floor; a small branch library for the surrounding inner-city community is on the second, along with staff lounge and offices, an auditorium and a carpeted "environment" for preschoolers. To maximize the amount of space available for storage of the books and cassettes, the two floors become three for the stacks.

The design is meant to be a "study in reversals and inversions," according to Tigerman. "The bulk of the building is made up of baked enamel panels that are light weight in character but are made to appear opaque, while the building's hypotenuse that is concrete and dense is made to appear transparent," Tiger-man said. This is accomplished by the use of minimal fenestration—a few porthole windows—on the metal panels that help give them an appearance of extreme weight. In contrast, the undulating window on the concrete facade helps disguise its real weight. The concrete wall acts as a great beam for the 165-foot window, which repeats the shape of the interior circulation path and has been described as a "willful act of irrationality." Said Tigerman, "Blindness is irrational, as is the window." Further playfulness comes into the exterior by the use of an abstract portal, which marks the entrance to the parking lot, and a two-car garage in the shape of an automobile is parked in the lot.

Philip Turner

Soft corners and a linear plan.

Upon entering the library, the patron first reaches the control desk, with the volunteer reading room to the right and the lounge with plug-in monitors for cassettes to the left. Beyond is the Braille catalog and circulation counter. The swerving circulation counter runs the entire length of the first floor, is cut away underneath to allow the wheelchair bound to move out of the way and dips where staff persons can be found, with the deepest dip being the circulation desk.

The ruling concept behind the first floor is a linear plan that can be followed and memorized most easily without sight. Also, all the furniture is built-in so its location can be easily learned and all surfaces are soft-cornered to reduce harm from collision.

On the second floor, the tiny staff lounge is subdivided into different levels of seating areas "to accommodate feuds," in Tigerman's words. The wall surrounding the auditorium is rippled. On both floors exposed pipes, ducts, brackets and wires are brightly painted. Color inside and out is intended "to create a colorful focal point to the otherwise drab, deteriorating inner-city neighborhood," in Tigerman's words.

The jury commended the building for responding "to the users' particular needs in an innovative and evocative manner. . . . The atmosphere of the entire project suggests that a building can be joyful and even capricious while still solving the pressing needs of a difficult and sensitive program."

Architect: City Architect, City of Chicago, Joseph W. Casserly. Consulting architect: Stanley Tigerman & Associates, Chicago. Client: Chicago Public Library/Chicago Public Library System. Structural engineer: Ray Beebe. Mechanical and electrical engineer: Wallace & Migdal. General contractor: Walsh Construction Co.

Howard Kaplan

Lounge with plug-in monitors for cassettes is located near the first floor entrance, top. A dip in the circulation counter indicates where a staff person is located, middle. Two-car garage shaped like an automobile in the parking lot, left.

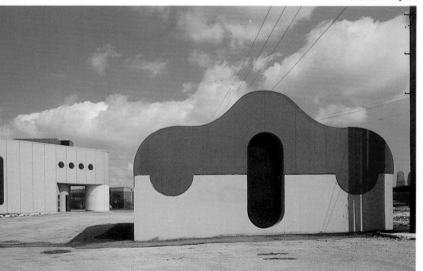

Howard Kaplan

Infill Apartments Respectful To Two Differing Contexts

The problem was to design an infill building on a very steep, constrained site on San Francisco's Russian Hill. The site, which had been undeveloped since before the 1906 earthquake, is bordered on the uphill side by a pedestrian street, Macondray Lane, and on the downhill side by a busy thoroughfare, Union Street. Buildings on both side lots edge the lot lines.

The solution by Hood Miller Associates, San Francisco, was to split the 13-unit residential condominium complex into two buildings, one uphill from the other. This preserved the existing pattern of midblock open space, allowed sunlight to enter the central garden and avoided blockage of views from nearby buildings. A stairway and glass-enclosed elevator connect the two buildings, which occupy the entire site due to a system to tiebacks under the neighboring structures.

The two facades are quite different in character and reflect their respective surroundings. The Union Street front is formal and symmetrical, echoing the pattern of Victorian facades throughout the block. On Macondray, there is a two-story informal, open-aired atrium as the entrance. Residents and visitors can enter either way, although access to the parking lot is only from Union Street.

The floor plans are somewhat unusual for a speculative building in that only the first two floors have similar layouts. The variation in floor plans was actually a "by-product of the need for upper floor setbacks," the architect suggests. "The uniqueness of the units result in condominiums that resemble 13 single family homes, worked like a Chinese puzzle into an envelope that harmonizes with the surrounding neighborhood."

Client: Hood Miller Properties and Farjam Corporation. Structural engineer: Shapiro Okino Hom & Associates. Mechanical engineer: J. W. McClenahan Co. Electrical engineer: Stehle Electric. Landscape architect: Paul Leffingwell. General contractor: Ralph Larsen & Son Inc. Completed in 1980.

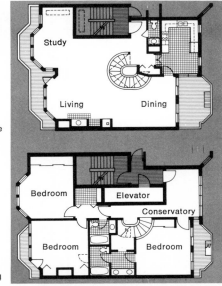

West penthouse

Lower level

North penthouse

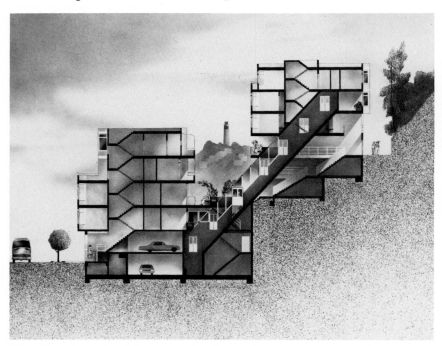

The 13-unit condominium complex, located on a steep hill, is split into two levels connected by a glass-enclosed elevator, above and across page. Only the first two floors of this speculative building have similar layouts, right.

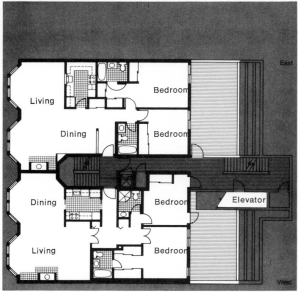

Living level I

Photographs by Richard Sexton

Splitting the building allows sunlight to enter the central garden and avoids blockage of views from nearby buildings, left and above.

The entrance on Macondray Street is a two-story informal, open-aired atrium, facing page. A curved staircase connects the two floors of the west penthouse, right. Dining room of the north penthouse, above.

Bringing Back an Art Deco Banking Hall

In the heart of Des Moines stands a five-story art deco jewel, the Valley National Bank. Designed in 1931 by Proudfoot, Rawson, Souers & Thomas (now Brooks Borg & Skiles), it was to be a base for a 27-story tower that never gained its full height due to the Great Depression. Vacant for five years during the mid-'70s, the building fell into a state of disrepair. Restoration of the building by Charles Herbert & Associates, Des Moines, returned it to its original splendor.

The exterior consists of fluted limestone walls that rest on a one-story base of polished granite. Granite also frames a deep, three-story entrance recess decorated with brass and bronze. During restoration the limestone was repointed and waterproofed,

the granite cleaned and the bronze and brass polished or oxidized and then lacquered. The ground floor storefronts were given a uniform treatment, which was lacking in the original design.

Inside, the lobby leads to central escalators that rise to the two-story banking area and adjacent double height loan department. In the main area 60 teller counters have been reduced to an eight-teller row on one side (using the best portion of the original counter). The heavy drapes that once adorned the windows have been removed and silver reflective glass has been added to control light and solar gain. Lead stencils, placed between two layers of glass, were cleaned, repaired and restored. The nickel chandeliers were cleaned and restored, although eight six-foot-high cylinders aimed at the white ceilings are the main light sources. Restoration of the plaster reliefs on the ceilings and walls was directed by Svend Paulsen (who won an AIA/AFL-CIO craftsmen of the year award in 1979 for this effort).

The jury said that the restoration was "undertaken with a great deal of design restraint as well as thorough technical competence." The general contractor for the project was the Weitz Co. Completed in 1979.

Among the original art deco touches are the lobby elevators and lead stencils embedded in the windows, above and left. Below, the main banking area with its nickel chandeliers and teller counter.

Block Returned to Its Original Character

One of the few commercial structures illustrating the stylistic influence of the Prairie School in Oak Park, Ill., is the Masonic Temple building designed in 1908 by E. E. Roberts. When the property became vacant in 1976, the village, which is known as a living museum of the Prairie School because of the many buildings designed by long time resident Frank Lloyd Wright, purchased it and offered financial incentives to developers to rehab the building and thus save it from demolition.

The structure was subsequently acquired by a large insurance company that hired the Office of John Vinci Inc., Chicago, to restore and adapt it for its corporate headquarters, as well as provide rental retail and office space. The architect restored the ground floor store fronts to their original appearance by removing the black Vitrolite facing that was added in the 1930s. The central recessed entry with its iron and glass canopy was recreated. A one-story wing that was added to the original building in 1914 gained a new limestone facade to differentiate it from the 1908 structure and to create a "harmonious continuity" with other buildings on the street.

The interiors, which had been gutted in the '30s by the previous owner (a department store), were renovated based on historical research and on-site investigations. An ornamental oak staircase that had been removed during the department store conversion was totally restored, based on a surviving section on the top floor.

Client: Industrial Fire & Casualty Co. Structural engineer: Charles E. Anderson. Mechanical engineer: R. M. C. West Inc. Electrical engineer: Meade Electric. General contractor: Ace Construction Corporation. Completed in 1981.

The 1908 design (above) was altered in the '30s with the addition of black Vitrolite facing (left). During the recent restoration, the Vitrolite was removed and the central recessed entry (right) and ornamental oak staircase (as seen in plan, above) were recreated.

Photographs by John Vinci/Phillip Hamp

112

Plain Suburban House Becomes Something Else

The design problem of adding a new living room and garden wall to an ordinary two-story suburban house was solved by knitting elements together with new wall fragments.

The house is the Schulman residence, Princeton, N.J., and the architect is Michael Graves, also of Princeton. In the redesign of the front facade and entrance, Graves linked three separate fronts horizontally and progressively decreased their size (the largest being the original house with a new entrance, the second the new facade for the living room and the third shielding the garden). In each segment colors and shapes are repeated. The concept behind this design, in the architect's words, is "as each segment steps forward in plan, the dimensions of the lapped siding increase in the elevation, thereby setting up a forced perspective that accentuates the new entry in the street facade." The house is of conventional wood frame construction, finished on the exterior with painted transite panels and clapboard, wood trim and stucco.

Of the facade's coloring Graves has written: "An attempt was made to root the building in the ground by placing the representation of the garden, dark green, at the base of the facade. Next, a terra-cotta band of belt coursing has been employed to register the idea of the raised ground plane or ground floor within the house. The green facade is continued above to suggest that addition as a garden room. To reinforce this ephemeral aspect, the color has been given a lighter value so that it appears to have been washed with light when seen in contrast to the darker green base. The composition is capped by a blue cornice with a second minor belting of terra-cotta, suggesting the juxtaposition of the second 'ground' (ceiling and floor) next to the reference to the soffit or sky."

Behind the garden wall is a new screened porch connecting the living room addition with the former garage, now used for storage. The fenestration of the living room wall is to be in "symmetrical relationship" with the gridded frame applied to the garage wall. The design of the fireplace repeats the layered motif found on the front facade and garden wall.

The color of the garden wall is "similar to that of the evergreen tree in the garden," Graves said, and the stepped form at the edge of the wall reflects the tree's shape. "The wall as receptacle of its form and color gives the tree a significant position it otherwise would not have. The position of the tree is seen as parallel to the position of man in his vertical stance, which it resembles. The garden wall in this case physically separates and yet metaphorically combines man and nature through its surface and formal treatment." Graves continued, "It is the polychromed wall as artifact that allows the full range of thematic significance. It is because the wall has lost its neutrality, has taken on figural qualities through the elaboration of form and color that we are able to make the connection between ourselves, the architecture and nature."

The jury called Graves' solution "impressive" in "proportion, composition, intricate color development and sensitivity to light conditions. . . . The complexity of the design achieves a relationship whereby it is not thrown at visitors but addressed to them." The jury noted that the house fits unobtrusively into its neighborhood context. The project was also commended for both its "inventive solution to an ordinary problem" and "the manner in which the physical environment was extended beyond the existing conditions."

Job captain: Caroline B. Constant. Client: Mr. and Mrs. Melvin A. Schulman. General contractor: Eduardus Goossen. Completed in 1979.

The redesign linked three separate front facades horizontally, facing page. This page, the new living room and garden wall, as compared to the old.

Photographs by Phillip MacMillan James

Pointed House Turns Its Face to a Lake View

The design of the LeJeune residence, Orono, Minn., was primarily determined by its site. Located on a peninsula at the western end of Lake Minnetonka (20 miles from downtown Minneapolis), the irregularly shaped site has 230 feet of lake frontage, approximately 350 feet at the street and depths from 80 to 195 feet. In addition to site constraints, strict covenants on the property required a low profiled, sloped roof structure built of "natural" materials to conform to the design of neighboring buildings.

Designed by Frederick Bentz/Milo Thompson/Robert Rietow, Inc., Minneapolis, the plan that evolved for the client, a couple with one young child and three grown children, is an elongated triangular building, whose roof rises in three progressive tiers. It begins in the front corner as one and a half stories and ends at a high wall at the lake side enclosing the two-story

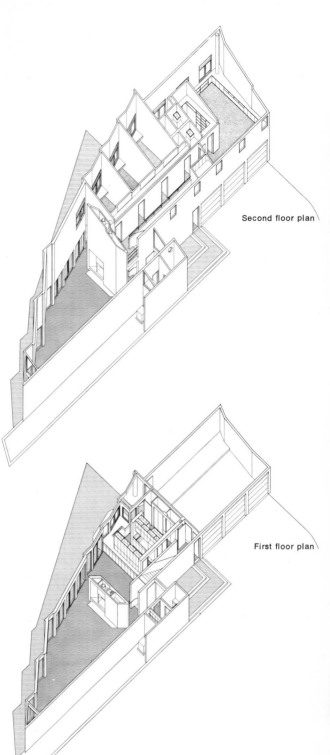

Second floor plan

First floor plan

The back of the house with its three-car garage faces the wind, below. The living room as viewed from the entrance, below. And the north corner with windows facing the lake, left.

living room and bedroom areas. The high wall is shaped with straight line segments in a gently bowing form to provide a single large bay window that looks out over a deck toward the lake.

The house turns its back against the northwest winter winds and the street traffic. The roof, which starts low at the windward side, deflects the breezes. Major windows are to the southeast, the entrance to the southwest and small windows to the north. All of the windows are double glazed.

Inside, the major living areas are arranged around a fireplace, which the architect calls a "form designed predominantly to be the pivot point of the formal organization of the plan." Along with a prefabricated fireplace unit, it contains a bar, closet at the second floor, the major vertical mechanical duct and riser space for the furnace flue from the basement. The fireplace also

separates the living from dining room, which in turn leads to the kitchen, utility room and three-car garage. The second floor houses three bedrooms, the master bedroom and bathrooms.

The house is finished on the outside with four-inch vertical cedar boards, stained light gray, and cedar shingles on the roof. The interior wall finish is white painted sheetrock except for the cedarboard covered fireplace.

The jury called the residence "a subtle response to a demanding site. Circulation sequences and careful placement of openings dramatize views to the lake while sheltering private spaces from road disturbances."

Client: Mr. & Mrs. Larry LeJeune. Structural engineer: Meyer Borgman & Johnson, Inc. General contractor: Cramer-Weir Construction Co. Completed in 1979.

117

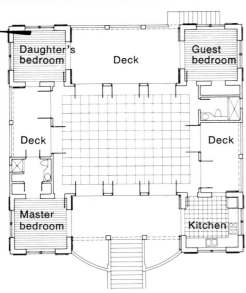

'Four-Poster' House on A Tropical Plantation

Located on the former site of the main house of a copra plantation in Nevis, West Indies, the Talbot house reflects the area's indigenous architecture. It is made of cut native stone and wood and painted in the customary complementary colors. While many houses have green roofs, this one is red, but both have been traditionally regarded as "neighborly." And the design, like others on the island, was clearly influenced by the architectural style brought during British colonization.

The house consists of four cut stone, two-story squares that define a central pavilion. The major concept of the design by Taft Architects, Houston, (John J. Casbarian, Danny Samuels and Robert H. Timme, partners-in-charge) was to "establish a sense of family structure that necessitated entering communal spaces prior to entering private areas," in the architect's words. This was accomplished by locating the bedrooms on the second level in three of the corners. The fourth houses the kitchen. Between the four corners are open-air porches, with the two bathrooms located next to the bedrooms on opposite ends of the north/south porches. The entrance is marked by a sweeping staircase. The "pavilion" with its high ceiling is one open room serving as the combined living and dining area. Ground floor corners are used as garages and workrooms, and a 35,000-gallon cistern located below the main living pavilion provides the water supply.

Color is used to enliven. On the exterior blue-green and cream colors adorn the shutters, panels and trim. Each room is painted with a different pair of complementary colors, and bands of floral patterns encircling the ceilings were hand-stenciled by the architect.

There is no mechanical temperature conditioning or electricity. The open decks providing exposure in all directions plus the use of oversized casement windows allow for cross ventilation regardless of wind direction. Power for lights, food preparation,

A sweeping staircase on the house's western side leads to the front porch and living area beyond (above, left). Sunlight through wooden slats makes patterns on the north side porch (left).

119

The pavilion houses the major living/dining area, below. Its ceiling is outlined by a band of hand-stenciled flowers, right. The master bedroom and pavilion open onto the front porch, facing page.

A strong and colorful composition.

appliances and refrigeration is provided by kerosene. The porches are shaded by wood slats.

"This house uses materials, forms and colors in a direct and bold manner, creating a strong composition of bright colored roofs against the mountain background," the jury commented. It praised the "simple details, well-proportioned rooms and subtle variety of interior paint colors."

The client, Mr. and Mrs. Thomas Talbot, are maple sugar farmers from Vermont who now cultivate island crops and spend many months in the West Indies. Their new plantation (the original on this site was built in the mid-1700s) is on a 10-acre site halfway up Nevis Peak on the small volcanic island that overlooks the Caribbean. General contractor was the Noral Lescott Construction Co. Completed in 1981.

Traditional Saltbox Form Expanded, Elaborated

The design of a summer and weekend residence for a family of five in East Hampton, N.Y., responds to both the architectural tradition of the area and to the client's specific programmatic requirements.

Designed by Eisenman Robertson Architects, Jacquelin T. Robertson, FAIA, principal-in-charge, New York City, the house formally is a response to the general "manners of a historical summer residential colony," in the architect's words. The design borrows from the New England salt box, which itself has been modified over the years to become a more leisurely summer cottage with the addition of porches, inglenooks, sun decks, etc. Says Robertson, "The house is a conscious attempt to employ these images so as to fit into a popular, genteel and still valid visual and social environment." The architect used materials, massing, scale of openings, trim color, roof silhouette and siting that relate to the surrounding buildings of similar style.

The house's layout responds specifically to the client's requirements that the children and guest quarters be separated from the adult area and that the public spaces be apart from the more private ones. Robertson achieves the former vertically; the latter horizontally.

On the ground floor there are two major "public" areas; the dining/kitchen/television room opens onto a raised, wind sheltered terrace with adjoining two-story entry hall. Off the hall are the children's bunk rooms and guest suite. Their quarters have access to the parking service court through a bathroom, which is to minimize "tracking" through the house.

The second floor houses a suite of interconnected rooms: the master bedroom and dressing room, a living room and inglenook that opens out to an enclosed porch. From the living room,

Photographs by Edmund H. Stoecklin

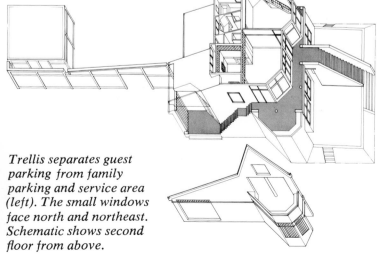

Trellis separates guest parking from family parking and service area (left). The small windows face north and northeast. Schematic shows second floor from above.

123

Photographs by Edmund H. Stoecklin

Variety and 'a pleasing intimacy.'

bedroom and enclosed porch there are views of the dunes and ocean beyond. From the master bedroom, stairs lead to a small painting studio on the third floor that in turn overlooks the double-height living room. And for added privacy, the second floor has its own covered staircase off the front porch.

For protection against the prevailing cold winter winds, the house turns its back to the north, with small windows on the north and northeast facades. The larger windows that face south are protected with overhangs to reduce glare and summer heat. West-facing windows are pulled back behind an outer wall to further control strong, west light. Floor-through ventilation promotes summer cooling.

The exterior cladding and roof is of cedar shingles; the decks are of redwood, and interior walls and ceilings are sheetrock with painted pine trim and shelving. The floors are oak, except in the kitchen and entry areas where they are Mexican brick tile. Entry walls and terrace are of paving brick. Family parking and the service area are separated from the guest parking by a long rose-covered trellis. The service court is accessible through a coat and mudroom off the front hall.

Of the house, the jury commented, "its silhouette makes a bold but harmonious impact in its expansive landscape, yet its variety of scale and texture creates a pleasing intricacy appropriate in a summer house."

Structural engineer: Robert Silman. Mechanical engineer: Martin Lewin. Electrical engineer: Carroll Cline. General contractor: M. Clarke Smith. Completed in 1979. □

Among the second floor rooms: the inglenook as seen from the living room, top, and the living room, left. Facing page, the porch at the southwest corner overlooking the driveway.

*Bunk beds in the children's rooms,
below, are located on the first floor.
Right, the two-story entry hall.*

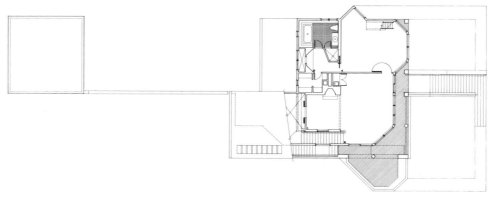

Second floor

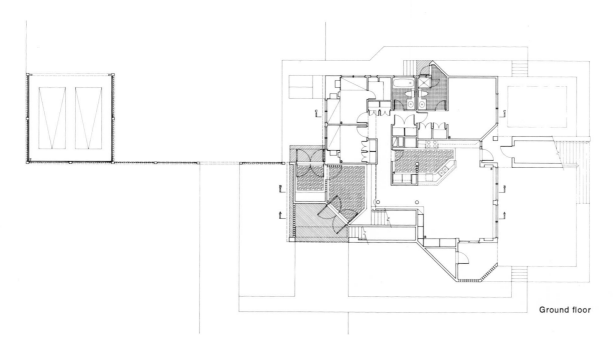

Ground floor

127

to its pyramidal shape, but to the fact that it is built in one of the city's valleys and creates an artificial peak that destroys the landscape identity of the "natural" San Francisco. Had the developer and architects respected the existing landscape identity they might have chosen another site or another form in which to establish the corporate identity of Transamerica.

The architect of the future *should* be encouraged to experiment with different structural forms. The John Hancock building in Chicago, in its truncated pyramidal form, is an example of a modern urban structure that lends distinctiveness as well as grace to the urban environment. The John Hancock building, in contrast to the higher Sears tower, immediately says "Chicago" to the arriving traveler who, in the 20th century, customarily comes by air and sees this landmark even above the clouds that often hang over Chicago. But the reason the John Hancock building is unobjectionable whereas the Transamerica building is objectionable is that the Hancock building enhances Chicago's landscape identity as the city of energy, enterprise and power (even though no longer merely the "hogbutcher for the world . . . stormy, husky, brawling city of the big shoulders," in Carl Sandburg's phrase). Chicago is a city that rises on a flat plain along the shore of a great lake. Chicago must create its verticality; San Francisco already has its own.

The search for relief from the monotony of square boxes and glass towers is perhaps most noticeable on New York's Manhattan Island, another place of power and energy built on a flat rock surrounded on all sides by water and expressing its spirit even more than Chicago by the exuberance of its upward growth. Where earlier the "less is more" boxes delighted and exalted by their very contrast with the Beaux-Arts formalism of their neighbors, with the proliferation of the former and elimination of the latter, the urban dweller, the architect and the planner have gradually been overwhelmed by ennui and anxiety. Is this the brave new world of the future? The liberating, unique structures of the postwar years have become faceless cogs in the coercive urban environment of the present.

No wonder some of the very architects who designed our present urban environment are seeking to humanize and historicize it: witness Philip Johnson's Chippendale-topped AT&T building. The diehard supporters of the earlier architectural revolution cannot decide whether Johnson is playing a whimsical joke on us or on AT&T. In fact he is reflecting a trend to liberate ourselves from ourselves and the revolution we have created. The more probable avenue of escape will be through unusual vertical shapes (sometimes justified by the technological im-

Washburn *from page 89*

landscape identity of the places in which they build. Perhaps it was inevitable that the wave of the future hit San Francisco first. It is a city with dramatic natural features, though more modest in size than those of Rio, Vancouver or Los Angeles. The ability of man and his technology to dominate, manipulate and redefine the natural environment became apparent in San Francisco before it did in other cities. As a result of controversies growing out of this fact, San Francisco developed and incorporated in its urban design plan a comprehensive statement of how its skyline should look. But the plan was adopted only *after* San Francisco's graceful skyline was, in the words of Richard Hedman, the city's current urban design chief, "lost forever, a victim, you might say, of rationalized vandalism."

San Francisco's urban design plan of 1971, which emerged from the controversies over the insertion of the massive Bank of America and the pyramidal Transamerica buildings into the urban fabric (above), boldly asserted the need to establish a re-

lationship between a building's size and shape to (1) its visibility in the cityscape, to (2) important natural features and to (3) existing development. The guidelines, as Allan B. Jacobs, Hedman's predecessor, has put it, "called for tall buildings, unlimited in height, to be clustered in and around downtown, in a hill form, to reflect but be separate from the natural topography of the city." At the same time, "tall buildings were also called for on some of the hilltops, on Nob and Russian hills, for instance, to emphasize hill forms and to safeguard views. . . . Buildings of smaller scale were to be located at the base of hills and in the valleys between them. Where existing hilltop development was low, or where hills were capped with open spaces, new buildings would also remain low to preserve the natural slope of the hill and to maintain public views. Building heights were to taper down to the shoreline of the bay and ocean." San Francisco's Urban Design Plan was as sensitive to bulk as it was to height.

The objection to the Transamerica building, under such guidelines, is not peratives of solar power and other forms of energy collection) rather than by nostalgic trips into the past, but there seems no question that the mindless repetition of the classic urban box (of which the Avenue of the Americas is the "bad" example) is now perceived as a bore and all architects will be searching for forms that liberate us from the monotony imposed on us by the mass adoption of the box in the 1950s and 1960s.

Perhaps the critical lesson that the architect must learn, and is in the process of learning, is that the contrast between nature and structure is no longer relevant. Nature is structure and structure is nature. Indeed, whether we are talking of man, rocks, trees, cement, ocean or stars, we are talking of a unity that began its path of differentiation with the "big bang" by which the universe came into being. We are all elements of the same basic material building blocks, of which carbon is the principal, whether we are the builder or the built. That unity is increasingly recognized: the subsequent differentiation is being perceived as a matter of form rather than of principle. The architect can either lead the way into shaping his materials in conformity with this understanding, or he can be dragged kicking and screaming into a coerced acknowledgment by the political authorities under whom he must ultimately function.

I believe architects are today what poets were in earlier generations: form givers and seers. Of course, there are good architects and bad ones, just as there were good and bad poets. But the poet earlier and the architect today see further than their fellow citizens because they are in closer touch with the ultimate reality, whether spiritual or material. I, for one, am confident that the architect will lead, not follow, mankind.

John Feild: Judging urban buildings on the basis of 'their impact on their environment and on the people who use them.'

When you add the word "urban" to architecture you have changed the name of the creative challenge. Urban architecture is both qualitatively and quantitatively more complicated than designing free-standing buildings like the pyramids or a resort hotel or a Fallingwater house in the woods. Each new urban building either anticipates its environment or changes the one it is plunked down into. There is no way it can avoid changing the patterns of living of very large numbers of people. Urban buildings have "impact" and, in a sense,

it is their impact on their environment and on the people who use them that offers us a better way to judge their quality and their value than normative or historical design and esthetic standards.

I make this suggestion because, as a layman and a long-time urban politician, I am perhaps more sensitive to the "complications" of urban architecture than I am purity of design. From where I sit, the architecture/design of an urban building must be looked at by both private investors and city officials not only in terms of how well its form relates to its function but also how well it relates to the present or future environment in which it will be built and how well it will serve the interests and needs of the people who will be using it. The urban factors that influence the design/function aspect of the building are both financial and political.

The critical cost constraints on the design (leaving aside matters of esthetics) are shaped by the financing available from either private or public sponsors. The private investor will be influenced either by the anticipated return on his investment or the benefit to his enterprise, as in the case of corporate buildings. The government sponsor is influenced first by the condition of the economy, next by the present and historical (debt) ratio between the jurisdiction's revenues and expenditures and finally by the political commitment and judgment of the administrators and elected officials who vote to spend the taxpayers' money. Both private and public sectors are influenced by the availability of land, the zoning issues that may be involved, the need for clearance, public acquisition or the possibilities of disposal of public land or facilities.

The environmental/design constraints imposed on the design of urban buildings include height limitations, density ranges and surrounding mobility (roadways, parking, public transportation, skywalks, etc.). All of these become political issues when urban buildings are involved, and they influence the design, often negatively.

The people/design constraints imposed on urban buildings relate to the number of people the building will serve, the range of their interests, whether the building should be single use or multiple use (this is a public policy issue), the factors affecting access to the building and the amenities the building and its site should/could provide in terms of open space and public services.

These are but a few of the factors that conspire to challenge architects who de-

John Feild is one of Washington's most authoritative consultants on urban affairs and editor of the public policy newsletter *The Feild Report*. For many years he was on the staff of the U.S. Conference of Mayors.

sign urban buildings. It is the degree to which they have all been surmounted that produces the building's "impact." And, it seems only fair to me, those who would judge the urban architect's achievements must likewise take such complicating factors into account.

In this spirit and from this perspective, let me list nine buildings in three categories that seem to me to have had more than usual "impact" on the cities where they were built.

Starting with city halls. There are, of course, more old ones than new ones. Among the old, I like the solid grandeur of the Milwaukee "Hall" tower (below). Built in 1895, it has been fully restored in recent years by Mayor Henry Maier and continues to symbolize the sturdy government that the voters of the city have been returning to office for over 24 years. (Mayor Maier's tenure now exceeds that achieved by the late Richard J. Daley, Chicago's previous big-city champ.) Among the new buildings, it is hard to beat Boston's City Hall for impact. My third selection, although technically not a city hall, is the new Hennepin County building in Minneapolis, which gave the city a center that its old city hall did not.

Next, culture. Here again, there are more old buildings than new—museums, opera houses, theaters, concert halls and science centers. I'll stick to the newer buildings. For sheer impact, Washington's Kennedy Center for the Performing Arts has probably had more influence on the life of the city than New York's Lincoln Center has on its community because the nation's capital has never been and is not likely to be its cultural capital. But Lincoln Center is New York. There are three other cultural buildings that have had real impact that come to mind—Milwaukee's Music Center, Los Angeles' Dorothy

Chandler Pavilion and San Francisco's new Symphony Hall. On the ground that it added more to its community than the others did to theirs, I pick Milwaukee for my third choice.

Civic centers are more difficult. There are more bad ones than good ones. Almost all of them have site problems. Many are underutilized. Here are three of good design that I think have had a beneficial impact on their cities: Fresno, Calif.; Norfolk, Va., and Baltimore.

Civic centers spawn hotels. But the best designed hotels are not always near them. The Regency Hyatt in Atlanta was a unique statement. It had impact. But, in a town where hotels have been one of its major industries since the turn of the century, it is harder to have impact in Chicago. The Ritz-Carlton came to town and pulled it off.

Center city revival has had uneven success in the past three decades. I don't think I would get much argument, however, if I picked Ghiardelli Square in San Francisco, Faneuil Hall marketplace in Boston and Harborplace in Baltimore as super contributors to new urban vitality.

Then, there is the contribution of corporate headquarters buildings to the urban environment, provided, of course, your city is lucky enough to have a rich corporation in its midst. New York, Chicago and Pittsburgh are overwhelmed with them. I'll leave them to others. How about these three? The IDS Building in Minneapolis, the Levi Strauss headquarters in San Francisco (page 34) and the Toledo Trust Company's headquarters building in Toledo, Ohio's emerging Maumee riverfront development.

What about the design quality of large scale commercial development that has emerged in some cities and has revitalized others? An older model would be the Golden Triangle in Pittsburgh. A newer model would be Houston. Even though I am bothered by its unexpectedly negative impact on the older downtown area, one would have to pick Detroit's Ren-Cen for its Land of Oz qualities.

For historic restoration, I suppose Charleston, S.C., Savannah, Ga., and the Vieux Carré in New Orleans would be on everyone's list. But the Pabst Theater in Milwaukee, the Pantages Theatre in Tacoma (in process) and Symphony Hall in Cincinnati might not. They ought to be.

When it comes to airports, Eero Saarinen's Dulles International is in a class by itself. You have to be a jogger or a long distance walker to cope with most American airports. Most of them are expensive disasters. Not so Dulles. Tampa comes next and St. Louis is still a jewel.

I'll conclude with three architectural special mentions that have had unusual impact on their urban environment: Saarinen's St. Louis Gateway Arch, the Chi- cago Circle campus of the University of Illinois and the scattered highrise housing buildings for the elderly in Minneapolis.

Obviously, I've left out a great many important, well designed urban buildings that others would probably and rightly claim have had more impact on their city's environment than my choices. Nobody's perfect.

Itzhak Perlman: 'When it comes to accessibility the trend is disappointing.'

I do not pretend to know much about trends in architecture in general or American architecture in particular. As a performing artist, my experience with architecture is limited to airports and concert halls, although I do confront other structures such as public buildings, hotels, etc. Because I am disabled, the first thing I notice about any building is whether or not it is accessible. When it comes to concert halls, I notice several things: the acoustics, the esthetics and the accessibility.

I am sure that it is obvious to you by now that accessibility is the number one problem that I'm concerned with. Let me talk about concert halls: I do not feel that there has been any trend, one way or another, either acoustically or esthetically. It's a hit or miss situation, obviously depending on the architect who designs the hall and the acousticians who work on it. However, when it comes to accessibility, the trend is disappointing. This situation is quite upsetting to me.

Everybody is aware of the various regulations concerning accessibility of public places in the U.S. If the structure is even partially supported by federal funds, it has to be made accessible. Regulation 504 specifically deals with that issue. However, I find that architects do not really understand the true meaning of accessibility. They figure that accessibility means being able to get into a building with no barriers. However, in many buildings it means going through the basement, through a garage door, getting on a freight elevator—in other words, the back-door treatment. This is not what accessibility is all about. There are few architects who understand this concept, the reason being that it is not taught in schools of architecture. I have spoken with I.M. Pei about the concept of "accessibility with dignity" and he agreed with me that it is something

Itzhak Perlman is an internationally acclaimed violinist. **Jane Blaffer Owen** helped found Historic New Harmony, Inc., to preserve historic buildings in New Harmony, Ind., and to encourage good new architecture there. The group is the recipient of a 1982 AIA medal.

that should be emphasized with greater care. Another element in architecture that is foreign to architects today is incorporating accessibility into their original artistic concept. Again, the reason for this lack of knowledge is a lack of education in the field.

Schools of architecture should emphasize these problems by offering required courses in barrier-free and universal design. Such courses would enhance the awareness of the architects and would present them with new challenges.

1981, the International Year of the Disabled Person, has come and gone, and one of its most important goals, the awareness of accessibility problems, should have been reached and was not. I just hope that schools of architecture throughout the country will help their students achieve that awareness. This will enhance the quality of life of America's largest minority, the disabled.

Jane Blaffer Owen: 'All that glitters here is not architectural gold.'

For the last 40 years, I have lived part of each year in houses built by Swabian German peasants. They brought to New Harmony, Ind., in 1814 the architectural style and practices that had served their ancestors for half a millennium or more. Our family home is in Houston—weather-beaten, New England architecture, and a venerable relic of a 1930 flood. In those days our sector of the Bayou overflowed and our land was a far outpost of the known Houston world. I mention this to establish my uncontemporary background But a cat, I presume, can look at a queen, her parure and her courtiers. Developers, contractors and architects strive for advancement here as, perhaps, in no other city. Recent statistics indicate that Houston leads the nation in current construction.

But all that glitters here is not architectural gold. Glass skins are tinted baby blue, spearmint green, silver, gold and occasionally, a discreet brown. Excepting for Philip Johnson's Pennzoil building, our few truly distinguished buildings are of poured cement or stone—Ulrich Franzen's Alley Theater, I. M. Pei's Texas Commerce Bank, Obata's Neiman-Marcus. There are some excellent brick buildings at the University of Houston, and Ben Brewer's Capital National Bank —an aluminum building with a fluorocarbon finish that gives pleasure to the eye and doesn't astonish. There are some fine small buildings and residences done by architects, such as Howard Barnstone and Preston Bolton, also architect for the C. G. Jung Education Center.

As I write, some new colors are rising a few miles from the bastion of our woods, the dusty rose and tapered crayolas of Cesar Pelli's Four Leaf Towers. If an architect is asked to thrust human habitations 439 feet into the sky where hopefully people shall be better protected from theft and murder than they were in their former and fast vanishing neighborhoods, he might as well put a cheerful face upon it. Since your editor has asked me to project trends, I believe the evidence around me points to the greater use of color. The downtown branch of the YWCA presents an even wider range of color abstractions than do the Pelli towers. Though Michael Graves has not yet come to town, assuredly he will!

But, happily, James Stirling has visited us and left a superb example of British understatement, wit and wisdom at Rice's school of architecture. He was commissioned by architects to add a wing to their existing architectural department, and he easily cleared the difficult hurdles of such an assignment. He could have out-raced his neighbors by a much wider margin.

I heartily applaud the JOURNAL's mid-May 1981 cover choice. I am awed by Fay Jones' Thorncrown Chapel, as I have been by few contemporary churches. If there is, indeed, a shift away from Bauhaus black, white and gray, then I rejoice that Fay Jones depends on seasonal changes of trees, the shifting of clouds and the presence of stone for his coloration. The skillful filtering of natural light at intersections of ceiling trusses is done with the sensitivity of a Louis Kahn, whose Fort Worth Kimbell Museum is the jewel without price of our Texas architectural crown.

I devoured your photos and descriptions of this amazing structure, but did not read that it had a covered bridge for an ancestor. The family likeness, I feel, is there. If this church seeks to restore our lost unity with nature, I am afraid the Crystal Cathedral does not. I am an admirer and friend of Bob Schuller and doubt that his broad vision was served by his architect. An association, possibly irrelevant, springs to my mind. A decade or so ago, the Metropolitan Museum hosted an exhibit of the clothing of famous Hollywood stars. I could not possibly forget a dazzling silver sequin dress that once belonged to Marilyn Monroe. The great warmth and humanity and spiritual grandeur of Bob Schuller easily fills the great spaces of his cathedral. I can't help but wonder about the future of these spaces when he is no longer there. Will the cathedral become a beautiful and eye-catching gown on a lifeless manikin? Perhaps not.

If producing a family constitutes trend setting, I should mention that New Harmony's contemporary buildings have birthed healthy offspring. Philip Johnson's public architecture was not conspicuously

The multipurpose main room, focus of Evans Woollen's New Harmony Inn.

curvilinear until he was driven in a farm truck over the gentle hills and valleys of southern Indiana. Our topography introduced six interlocking circles into his canopy for the presiding lady of the Roofless Church, The Lipchitz Madonna.

Evans Woollen's pristine New Harmony Inn quickly attracted visits from the Benedictine monks of St. Meinrad's Arch Abbey, and secured for him a handsome commission. A new library, extensive dormitories and an octagonal chapter house, all reminiscent of the warm yet well disciplined architecture of Monte Cassini, will be dedicated soon.

Richard Meier had hardly finished his Atheneum and his studio for pottery before he was asked to design a school in Columbus, Ind. Interestingly, none of our New Harmony buildings depends on glass or color for their éclat. Their creators wrote their scores in close rapport with nature. Meier's western facade of the Atheneum follows the curve of the Wabash and his open spaces frame particular views of meadows and woods. Johnson's two courtyards for the Roofless Church help define a continually changing panorama of sky, and his classic portico overlooks a cornfield. Although these particular views are as American as our flag, particularly when the vertical rows of young corn are reaching upward, the Meier and Johnson buildings enjoy a dialogue in Greek when soft lights wash them at night and the fields are dark. Though Evans Woollen uses brick for his Entry House

and the Tillich Refectory, he has not missed a single opportunity to integrate man and nature at ground level.

Kevin Roche's Temple of Dendur Pavilion for the Metropolitan invites the participation of Central Park, graciously, and I believe Edward Barnes' large atrium for the new IBM building will refresh all who enter. However, Norman Gaffney's modest farmhouse at Coatsville, Pa., (by Bohlin Powell Larkin Cywinski) justly merits its AIA honor award and my few thoughts on future trends. This is an affordable, unpretentious home, not a house, and an honest love match between old structure and new, between man and nature. It is chamber music, not a symphony. Unless my hopes for America have grossly obscured my vision, I foresee fewer, grandly orchestrated new houses, and more solar heated small ones, built either from scratch or in league with older houses and buildings. Cities shall, presumably, continue to grow vertically and to store its people in unyielding condomiums. Worsening and insoluble traffic conditions will continue to push young families into suburban or rural areas. I have many young Houston friends who have already moved to the Brenham area and done so with taste and courage. Many more will follow. Although I did not see chickens or a tethered cow outside Mr. Gaffney's home, there was space for them. His building philosophy may point a way out for the young. I hope so, for they are on the firing line today. □

Cross-Sectional Selection of Award Winners from Around the Nation

The place to look for the state of the art of architecture is at the grass roots, where it is being built. So each year as part of our annual review we present a sampling of awards given by AIA's local, state and regional component organizations. It must be a sampling because there are hundreds of such awards each year. We don't try to second-guess the juries—our choices are made largely with the goal of getting a cross section of geographical areas, building types, and approaches. The buildings chosen this year are shown here and on the following pages. Text is by Nora Richter Greer, Allen Freeman, and Lynn Nesmith.—*Ed.*
Los Angeles Chapter. Sun-Tech Townhouses, Santa Monica, Calif. (above); Urban Forms/Steve Andre, Santa Monica. There are 18 four-level town houses on this 150x160-foot site, each with two bedrooms, den, two and one-half baths and a rooftop deck. A dynamic high-tech image was created by the use of ex-

posed chimney stacks, metal railings, bold shapes formed in the stucco walls and carefully positioned outdoor lighting. Large windows are strategically placed to admit natural light into two-story interior spaces, while maintaining privacy for each unit.

Los Angeles Harbor Department Administration Building, San Pedro, Calif. (right); John Carl Warnecke & Associates, Los Angeles. Planned as a catalyst for a redevelopment area in this port city, the office facility accommodates 350 management, engineering, accounting, security and clerical personnel with the capacity for an additional 100 employees. The building sits on top of a landscaped, terraced parking garage that was designed to blend with the surrounding multistory office and commercial buildings to the south and the two-story residences to the north. It is clad in glass and covered by weathering steel trusses and horizontal stainless steel guardrail cables.

Inland California Chapter. Vintage Club Cottages, Indian Wells (above); Patrick Evan Sheehy, Palm Springs. Six cottages are clustered in a fan-shaped pattern facing outward toward a golf course and sharing a landscaped courtyard and parking area. The architect chose mauve sand-finished stucco, red brick window frames and Mexican barrel tile as finishes. In each of the 135 two- and three-bedroom units, the nine-foot ceilings have beam trellises.

Southwest Oregon Chapter. Spectra-Physics Manufacturing and Research Facility, Eugene (right); Moreland/Unruh/Smith, Eugene. This 54,000-square-foot building is the first phase of a master plan that called for an expandable facility to house various industrial, research and administrative services. The architect chose indigenous design materials and a low-profile building designed to reflect a "campus-like environment." Sloping windows deflect sound and light upward into the perimeter roof cove, which shields mechanical equipment from view.

Portland Chapter. Tualatin Hills Park and Recreation Complex, Beaverton, Ore. (above); Broome, Oringdulph, O'Toole, Rudopf & Associates, Portland. This recreation and sports facility, the largest in the state, includes an aquatic center, indoor and outdoor tennis courts, administrative offices, public service maintenance building, 500-car parking lot and football, soccer, softball and baseball fields. The architect clustered the buildings on a knoll of the 66-acre partially wooded site and buried the two major structures to reduce heating and cooling costs. Their earth berms also serve as bleachers for outside sports.

Addition to the William Temple house, Portland (below); Fletcher Finch Farr Partners, Portland. Housed for 10 years in an 1878 mansion, the Episcopal Lay-men's Mission Society needed additional space for "intense public use," such as meetings and counseling services. The two-story addition reflects the residential character and general forms of the original structure without duplicating its ornate detail. The exterior is finished with cedar shingles stained to match the slate of the existing building. A sandstone planter wall continues the line of an existing stone wall.

Dick Busher

Seattle Chapter. Fifth Avenue Theater renovation, Seattle, (above); R. F. Mc-Cann & Co., Seattle. This 2,100-seat theater was designed in 1926 as a vaudeville house, later was used as a movie palace and closed in 1976. In the renovation, interior ornamental detail was repaired, regilded and replaced to match the original surfaces as closely as possible. Row space was increased, seats rebuilt, the stage raised, downdraft airconditioning in-stalled, an electronic sound system added and sightlines improved. The theater will house touring Broadway plays, regional musical and dramatic productions and a resident ballet company. Acoustical capabilities and the size of the auditorium also make it suitable for chamber operas and recitals.

Northwest Region. Central Pre-Mix Concrete Co. Corporate Headquarters, Spokane, Wash. (below); Walker McGough Foltz Lyerla Architects, Spokane. Both levels of this 16,000-square-foot earth covered building receive natural light through continuous bands of windows along the south wall. A two-story atrium connects the upper and lower levels and separates the reception area from the executive offices. The HVAC system redistributes internal heat, stores excess heat for later use and utilizes outside air for cooling.

Photography Unlimited

Western Mountain Region. Writer Square, Denver (right); Bafker Rinker Seacat & Partners Architects, Denver. A mixed use development links the historic lowrise buildings of the Larimer Square area and the highrise office towers of downtown Denver. The project's scale changes from 11 stories on the downtown side to four stories on the other side. The complex includes a 10-story office tower, three- and four-story residential buildings, two levels of underground parking and an enclosed street level plaza with restaurants and shops. The new buildings have "traditional" brick arches and cornices and vertical windows.

Linton residence, Highland, Utah (below); Joseph Linton, AIA/Wayne Bingham, Salt Lake City. The clients, a family of seven, requested an energy efficient house whose design contrasted with the environment. Located on a sharp 20-foot vertical rise on the north end of a gently sloping cleared lot, the north exposure is built into the hill and the south exposure contains large windows for passive solar gain and unobstructed views of the Rocky Mountains. The house is clad in a shining silver metal curtain wall. And the availability of ground water accommodated a geothermal heat pump.

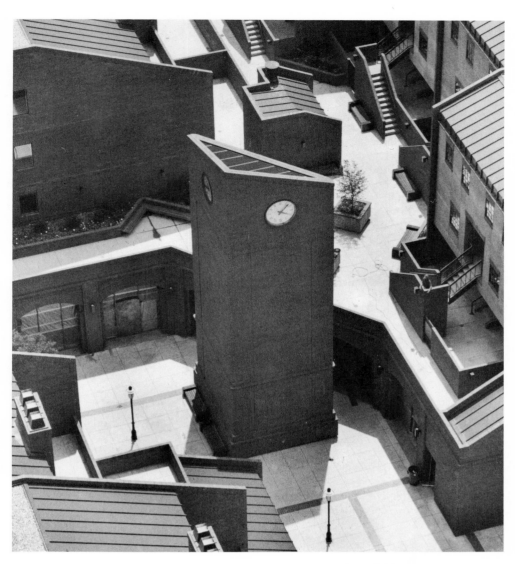

Western Mountain Region. Single family residence, Soda Creek, Colo. (right); Anderson Architects, Denver. The client wanted an energy efficient house that incorporated passive solar design concepts. The response is a 2,500-square-foot triangular house with a 29x17-foot passive greenhouse as the entry and a 42x17-foot water-wall on the south facade. The wood frame structure, located on a six-acre site 25 miles west of Denver, has a sand colored synthetic stucco exterior finish that matches the interior wall surfaces.

Utah Society. Benedictine Monastery, Schuyler, Neb. (below); Astle Ericson & Associates, Omaha. The program called for a facility with adjacent chapel, administrative offices, printing facilities, kitchen, dining room, library, guest quarters and adequate private living space for each member. The chosen site was 16 acres of rolling hillside four miles north of town. The architect designed a partially underground building for energy conservation and to blend with the natural contour of the land. A courtyard and chapel with two large skylights are located in the center of the facility. Wooden columns and beams are prevalent throughout the interiors.

Nevada Society of Architects. Truckee Meadows Community College, Reno (above); Dolven Larson Daniels, Reno. The program consisted of creating a "compact multilevel interrelated campus" through the addition of an energy efficient facility containing classrooms, administrative offices, community service programs, library and dining area that would be flexible for future additions. Directly adjacent to the existing building, the four-story steel frame structure has minimum exterior glazing with the majority of windows facing south, and is earth bermed. A three-story atrium with skylights that bring in natural light provides an informal gathering place for students and links the major functions of the college. A multizone HVAC mechanical system provides the heating and cooling requirements of the entire facility. The jury cited the project for "its harmonious solution to a very large, complex program on a difficult, sloping site."

Brown residence, Washoe County (below); Maurice J. Nespor & Associates, Reno. The architect was asked by a young couple to design a house heated by solar energy. The response is a 2,600-square-foot wedge structure allowing optimum slope for solar glazing and deflecting the valley winds. The wood-frame, three-bedroom house is set on a semi-remote mountain site with undisturbed views of desert landscape. The jury commented: "Thoughtful orientation and creative energy concepts provide for a unique and economical solution well adapted to the surrounding environment."

Nevada Society of Architects. Dickenson Library Addition, University of Nevada, Las Vegas (above); JMA Architects, Las Vegas. This four-story metal skin structure houses the university's library services, materials processing and administration and is linked by a bridge to the existing circular-shaped library now serving as a storage and cataloging area. The architect chose a rectangular building as the annex to complement the "strict geometry of the existing circular structure." The new building's entrances, "special function zones" and circulation areas are circular. Small windows are located in cutouts that provide protection from solar gain in the summer, and south and west exposures contain tinted skylights for natural daylighting.

New Mexico Society. Bird of Prey Exhibit, Rio Grande Zoological Park, Albuquerque (right); Van H. Gilbert, AIA, Albuquerque. The program called for an exhibit to display five species of birds in their natural habitat, yet provide privacy for breeding. Separate enclosures were required after research revealed that each species had particular needs for flying space, perch heights and materials, shade, sun, feeding areas and nesting sites and materials. The architect chose a curved shaped design that incorporates existing deciduous trees, native plant life and artificial rock cliffs with a southwest exposure.

Rick Gardner Photography

New Mexico Society. Hope Building, Albuquerque (left); Cherry/See Architects, Albuquerque. Built in 1894 as a doctor's office and residence, this two-story building is the second oldest structure remaining in downtown Albuquerque. Restoration of the facade included removing the stucco added in the 1950s; uncovering the large exterior arches; replacing, patching and repainting the brickwork and replacing the aluminum door and window frames. Interior walls were replastered and an oak wainscot was installed. A dropped light trough conceals the new mechanical and electrical systems.
Dallas Chapter. Charles Storey residence garden room addition, Dallas (below); Thomas, Booziotis & Associates, Dallas. The client requested a permanent space for entertaining that would "capture" the environment of a tent structure and complement the design of the present house. The architect chose a glass box edging the existing ledge stone piers. Natural and artificial light filter through hung vent-wood panels.

Wayne Thom

Dallas Chapter. Trailwood United Methodist Church, Grand Prairie, Tex. (above); Thompson Parkey Associates, Dallas. Four acres of prairie land in suburban Dallas serve as the site for this 3,500-square-foot church. Forms and materials are overscaled so that the church differs visually from the surrounding tract houses. The interior of the wood frame structure features prefab wood trusses. Fluorescent lights illuminate the upper levels of the sanctuary and provide exterior ornamental lighting at night. The overall design is meant to reflect early Christian basilicas and rural American pioneer churches.

Texas Society of Architects. Puffer-Sweiven Office and Warehouse, Stafford (below); Morris*Aubry Architects, Houston. Because the building was to be surrounded by an office-warehouse park and because the client wanted a visually pleasant working environment, the architect turned outside views inward toward four triangular courtyards. The courtyards are between a 35,000-foot diamond-shaped office area on one side and a square block of executive offices and warehouse space on the other. The courtyard pictured features an awning-covered deck and barbeque pit. The facility also includes a 150-seat auditorium, a product display area, an audiovisual room, a gymnasium and a putting green.

Texas Society of Architects. O'Donnell residence, Dallas (above); Frank Welch Associates, Midland. Designed for a family of four, the house is located on a sloping wooded site in suburban Dallas. The clients requested that the existing vegetation of the site be preserved and that the house be easily adaptable to entertaining. Three separate buildings are linked by open flat galleries at the second level. The main living spaces and the master bedroom are housed on the upper level with the daughters' bedrooms on the lower level. An upper level porch overlooks a terrace, pool, guest house and tennis court. The jury commented: "The house is seen as a single structure whose basic formality is softened and lightened by subtle asymmetries."

Mercy Hospital, Bakersfield, Calif. (left); CRS, Inc., Houston. This 86,000-square-foot addition completes the first phase of a 15-year master plan to eventually replace the entire hospital. The four-story building houses the entrance lobby, reception area and new facilities for emergency, radiology, surgery, sterile supply and admissions. A bronze glass window wall surrounds the atrium and provides exterior views for patients and natural light. Solar gain is minimized since the window wall faces north. The 194-patient care area will be linked to a series of "nursing pods" that will be developed in the second phase.

South Dakota Chapter. Ready Mix Concrete Plant, Sioux Falls (right); TSP, Sioux Falls. The renovation of the plant included increasing the capacity while maintaining continuous plant operations, accommodating computerized control of the plant's functions, increasing employee comfort, reducing traffic hazards and improving its outward appearance and site. The jury commented on "the highly functional design, well suited to the industrial process and the sculptured quality of the plant."

North Dakota Chapter. Northwestern Bank of Fergus Falls, Fergus Falls, Minn. (below); Foss Architects, Fargo. Located in a rural community, this 30,456-square-foot steel framed, brick veneer building is designed to project "a progressive image" yet maintain the "character" of the region. Cascading bubble skylights provide passive solar heating, enliven the entrance way and provide natural daylighting and views of the river. The bank's hot water requirements are met by electric pumps that transfer the heated air in the greenhouse to a 12,000-gallon storage tank.

Ronald Schemmel

North Dakota Chapter. Vacation home, Pelican Lake, Minn. (above); Foss Associates, Fargo. Several families with children wanted to share a year-round vacation house with sleeping accommodations for a large number of people. Since the house is located on a sloping lot on the north side of a Minnesota lake, the architect placed large windows on the south facade in nearly every room for natural ventilation, passive solar heat gain and

views of the lake. The slope also allows nearly 15 percent of the exterior walls to be protected by earth. Seven bedrooms, two 60-square-foot bunk rooms and a sleeping loft provide the requested sleeping arrangements.

Iowa Chapter. Pioneer Hi-Bred International Central Division Headquarters, Johnson (below); Charles Herbert & Associates, Des Moines. A central atrium running the length of the building is de-

signed as an "interior street" and separates the offices, conference room, reception area, employee lounges from printing facilities. A bank of windows on the south facade provides natural light and a view of the adjacent man-made lake. Exterior surfaces on the north side are solid brick, and a glass block wall screens the service and delivery areas. An exterior plaza doubles as a display area during yearly promotional expositions.

Iowa Chapter. Davies Amphitheater, Glenwood Lake-Park, Glenwood (above); Dennis W. Stacy, Dallas. Providing a fixed seating capacity of 730 for several types of outdoor performances and community activities, this facility serves a community of 5,600. Existing vegetation forms a backdrop for the stage, which was constructed on existing grade, as was the last row of seating, thus minimizing site preparation. The sides of the service buildings define the stage and act as its sounding board. A steel space frame system supports wood decking over the stage to provide an acoustically reflective surface and to shield the west-facing audience from the evening sun. A second vertically mounted steel space frame system, positioned at the rear of the fixed seating, serves as a lighting tower.

Wisconsin Society. Fauerbach Condominium Development, Madison (below); Bowen Williamson Zimmermann, Madison. The larger block of apartments is a four and one-half-story building, with parking below, sited on a through street across from existing warehouses. On the lake side, smaller scaled town houses step down to the water's edge. This arrangement allowed six different living unit types with many variations. On the street side, masonry was used to be compatible with the main artery's urban character. Siding materials and pitched-roof forms were adopted on the lake side to relate to the existing residential community.

Chicago Chapter. The Anti-Cruelty Society Addition, Chicago (above); Stanley Tigerman & Associates, Chicago. This is the second addition to a 1930s institutional building, which the architect felt tended to symbolize the most unpleasant aspects of the institution—a euthanasia center for unwanted animals. The new facade, therefore, is intended to suggest a friendly dog's face, and the exterior treatment —double hung windows, horizontal aluminum siding, prefinished gray, with white trim—to evoke a residential feeling. The intended message: Come in and adopt a puppy.

De La Garza Career Center, East Chicago, Ind. (left); Murphy/Jahn, Chicago. Infill panels of insulated steel and insulating glass attach to an aluminum frame in this vocational training center, sited between the residential and industrial sections of the city. The structure utilizes long span joists and truss girders supported by prefabricated fireproof pipe columns. At the short ends of the building the structure is left exposed, suggesting future expansion in those directions.

Chicago Chapter. Hyde Park Historical Society, Chicago (above); John Vinci, AIA, Chicago. The historical society purchased an abandoned 1894 passenger station in 1978. Renovation included completely rebuilding the interior, installing insulating glass windows to match the originals, tuckpointing the exterior masonry and restoring the wooden trim to its original color. A wood-burning stove was installed, in addition to a new heating system.

Northeast Illinois Chapter. Community and Senior Citizens Center, Huntingburg, Ind. (before below; restored right); W. Lockwood Martling Jr., AIA, Downers Grove and Don Bergstrom Associates, Hinsdale. In the exterior renovation of the town's 1896 former opera house/city hall, the missing bell tower and chimneys were reconstructed after research of old photographs, and the bracketed cornice, gutters, downspouts and windows destroyed by a fire in an adjacent building were replaced also. Adaptation of the interior will be undertaken when funds are available. The jury commended the architect for attention to detail and for appropriate use of color.

Indianapolis Chapter. Hammond Block, Indianapolis (left); Schmidt/Claffey, Inc., Indianapolis. This lively flatiron building had fallen on bad times: The roof leaked, causing damage to a major truss; chimneys had either fallen off or been removed, interiors had been significantly altered, and the entire building, including windows, had been spray painted red. Exterior restoration included chemical cleaning of the soft red brick, replacing arches and missing pieces of dentil work, refinishing detailing in sand-textured white to approximate the look of stone and reconstruction of the roofline sign. A significant interior adaptation was addition of a mezzanine to the 16-foot-high top floor, thus increasing leasable space.

Detroit Chapter. Franklin-Wright Settlements Camp, Orion Township, Mich. (below); Rossen/Neumann Associates, Southfield, Mich. The directors of the camp, a nonprofit facility for underprivileged children, commissioned the architect to provide a master plan, renovate existing buildings and design new ones on the 82-acre lakefront site. The platform shown, centered on an open hearth, is the camp's focus, intended to provide a sense of community. (It has been nicknamed "the pagoda" because of its four Oriental gateways.) The first new buildings, three cottages with six bunk rooms each, are finished in cedar shakes stained gray. Their fenestration includes child-height windows, and interiors have bright supergraphics.

Balthazar Korab

149

Michigan Society and Detroit Chapter.
Matilda R. Wilson Aviary Wing, Detroit Zoological Park, Royal Oak (right); Carl Luckenbach/Robert L. Ziegelman, Inc., Birmingham. The glazed U-shaped addition of aluminum extrusions provides a circulation system allowing visitors to see the entire facility in a continuous sweep without back-tracking. The configuration also provides a center flight enclosure to accommodate a giant condor, which must be segregated from other birds because of its predatory nature. The condor enclosure was achieved economically by stringing a net across the top of the space within the U. The addition permits a progression of differing environments from rain forest to marshland to plains.

Bell Town Houses, Birmingham (below), also by Carl Luckenbach/Robert L. Ziegelman, Inc. A century-old single family residence, designated as an historic structure, provided the vocabulary of white clapboard and peaked forms for three new adjacent town houses in this Detroit suburb. The four houses are arranged to form private interior courtyards off rear-oriented living spaces.

Glen Calvin Moon

Balthazar Korab

Michigan Society. ACO Incorporated headquarters, Farmington Hills (above); Smith, Hinchman & Grylls Associates, Inc., Detroit. A curving skylight the width of the building extends from the roof of the office section to the midlevel mechanical area, bringing daylight into the open-plan offices. The balance of the building is devoted to highly automated warehouse operations for this retail hardware chain. The building skin is white enameled metal panels, demountable to facilitate expected growth of the company. The building was placed so that expansion would do minimal damage to the partially wooded site.

Duluth Public Library, Duluth, Minn. (left). Gunnar Birkerts & Associates, Birmingham. Because it was desirable to house the library's main collection on a single floor (in photo), and that floor would be larger than the proposed building site, the architect extended the top floor over part of an adjacent plaza, which was also part of the design project. The two lower stories progressively diminish in size from the top, providing partial pedestrian shelter for the edge of the plaza and over much of the building's long, narrow site. The two lower floors contain the circulation desk, an adult browsing area, the children's collection, administration areas and public meeting rooms.

151

John Marschall

Architects Society of Ohio. The River's Edge, Dayton (above); Lorenz & Williams Inc., Dayton. Where high levees once restricted pedestrian access to the Miami River, this urban river park provides concrete terraces and ramps to help people negotiate the steep descent. Terraces are wide, offering places for people to gather, and they also serve as seating for up to 1,000 people for the amphitheater/stage below. Handrails are steel; the bridge is laminated wood.

Thwing Student Center, Case Western Reserve University, Cleveland (below). Don M. Hisaka & Associates, Cambridge, Mass. This tiered building with receding facade of reflective and transparent glass is a link between two buildings dating from the turn of the century. The new building contains a bookstore and an atrium that functions as the core of the three-building complex, which forms an expanded student union that is a new focal point of the campus. The old build-

ings were renovated to house student lounges and food service areas. Silhouetted in the photo is an archway from one of the adjoining buildings, serving as a symbolic gateway to the center. Pedestrian access is now from three sides of the complex, with service functions restricted to the fourth. Windows were reglazed with operable insulated units, with airconditioning restricted to special use areas. This was felt to suffice during the September-May period of use.

Thom Abel

152

Architects Society of Ohio. Bay Village Library, Bay Village (above); Dalton•Dalton•Newport, Cleveland. Sited on a corner lot bounded by a school and an open park, the community facility was designed to blend with a residential neighborhood of mostly traditional houses. The flattened brick arches over windows and doors are repeated inside the library over openings that line a central corridor separating the main stack areas from support functions. Mechanical equipment on a flat, central roof area is screened from all directions by half trusses on the roof.

Municipal Swimming Pool and Tennis Facility, Mentor (left). Wandel & Schnell, Columbus. The structures shown are concession and bathhouse buildings clustered in the center of the site. They are wood-frame, slab-on-grade construction with stained wood siding. Surrounding them are 50 and 25 meter pools, a diving well and spray and wading areas; four tennis courts; a basketball court, and a landscaped parking area. Mature trees on the site were saved to edge the tennis and basketball courts.

Tennessee Society of Architects. Vacation house, Bersheba Springs (above); Seab A. Tuck III, Nashville. A drawbridge and a crow's nest are two features of this leisure-time house for a large family. Sited on a wooded slope, the house sits on a concrete pedestal. Vertical concrete forms are lined on axis from drawbridge entrance through the central kitchen to a rear deck. The cross-axis wings comprise living spaces on the first floor and bedrooms above. The house is sheathed in tongue and groove western red cedar. Interior features for the children include a brass firepole, secret ladders and a basketball goal integrated with the balcony rail in the two-story living room, called the Great Hall.

Gulf States Region and Arkansas Chapter. Commissary, Little Rock Air Force Base, Ark. (below); Cromwell Truemper Levy Parker & Woodsmall, Little Rock. Daylighting was an important design determinant in this 91,200-square-foot military grocery store. The roof of the shopping area incorporates north-facing clerestories, and lighting fixtures are controlled by photoelectric cells and dimmers to augment the natural source. Calculations indicate an annual saving of 2,800 kilowatt hours from daylighting. Other conservation systems include heat reclamation from refrigeration equipment, circulation of spillover cold air from freezer cases and earth berms. The building skin is silver-colored porcelain enamel insulated panels; the column-free automobile entrance canopy (in photo) is spanned by a 200-foot-long Pratt truss, which is expressed by fenestration.

Gulf States Region. Hermitage Park Suite Hotel, Nashville (above); Gresham, Smith & Partners, Nashville. The 1909, 11-story Hermitage Hotel was closed in 1977 because of firesafety violations. Restoration/renovation by its new owners began two years later. After research of J. Edwin Carpenter's original plans, the public spaces and original materials—including Italian and Tennessee marble, granite, terra-cotta, cirassian walnut, decorative plaster and art glass—were restored. Decorative details were restored by hand and repainted in original colors determined from paint scrapings. The upper eight floors with small guest rooms were gutted and 14 suites per floor were created.

Old U.S. Mint, New Orleans (right); E. Eean McNaughton & Associates, Biery & Toups and Bernard Lemann, New Orleans. Built during the Jackson Administration, the building in the Vieux Carré district functioned as a mint facility until 1909, and until 1963 housed a variety of government functions. It was given to the State of Louisiana in 1965, and in the mid-'70s a study found it feasible for conversion to mixed museum/commercial uses, to be operated by the Louisiana State Museum. Because of the many adaptations to William Strickland's 1830s building, the renovation approach was to select and enhance elements from various periods. Minimal structural changes were made, and all changes are reversible, say the architects.

Bill LaFevor

Alan Karchmer / Architectural View

155

Florida Association. Shelley house, Dorado, Puerto Rico (above); Thomas S. Marvel, FAIA, of Torres • Beauchamp • Marvel y Asociados, Hato Rey, Puerto Rico. Located in a coconut palm grove next to the Atlantic Ocean, this house derives its form and feeling from two sources, says the architect: the "hacienda" living style of the turn of the century, and the Prairie School-influenced architect Antonin Nechodoma, who practiced in the Caribbean during that period. The plan is cruciform, with all of the circulation and principal spaces off the foyer. The center of the house is a covered terrace, two stories high. Construction is exposed reinforced concrete with horizontal accents of glazed tile.

Bouterse house, Coconut Grove (right); Bouterse Perez & Fabregas, Miami. Used as a professional's retreat and for entertaining, this house on a lot only 50 feet wide fronts the end of a short canal leading to Biscayne Bay. The side walls, eight feet from adjoining two-story houses, are unpenetrated but have irregular profiles to avoid heavy massing. Inside, sight lines are strongly directional toward a view of the canal. Walls are white, and there is free use of stucco, as well as tile, glass block and white plaster.

Florida South Region. Miami Biltmore Complex, Coral Gables (left); Ferendino/Grafton/Spillis/Candela, Coral Gables. This former hotel and country club was restored and adapted for use as a city museum/art center/restaurant/pro golf shop with the help of two U.S. Department of Commerce grants. Doors, windows, capitals, columns, rafters, gutters and moldings of the Beaux-Arts/Mediterranean '20s building were replaced or repaired to specifications in the original working drawings (original architect: Schultz & Weaver).

Baton Rouge Chapter. Baton Rouge Bank & Trust Co. branch bank, Baton Rouge, (below); Bobbie B. Crump Jr.; AIA, Baton Rouge. The client wanted a visually prominent building, so the architect sited it back from the street and increased its apparent size by painting its used brick exterior white, extending a courtyard wall and increasing the roof area. The courtyard expands the apparent size of the lobby, as do the raised ceiling and skylights. Interior materials include slate and tile flooring; walls of painted used brick, cypress paneling, vinyl coverings and ceramic tile, and acoustical tile and painted gypsum board ceilings.

157

Photographs by E. Alan McGee

Georgia Association. The Roswell Facility, Roswell (above); Heery & Heery, Atlanta. This is a complex of buildings for assembly and distribution of Herman Miller office furnishings. Completed so far are three buildings comprising about one-third of a projected one million square feet of production and office space on a 135-acre site. The production buildings are of steel joists and joist girders with skin of insulated metal panels faced with clear anodized aluminum on the exterior and white baked enamel on the interior. Said the jury: "Skillful handling of high-tech imagery with a sensitive attention to detail."

Spaces and Illusions exhibit, High Museum of Art, Atlanta (right); Heery & Heery, Atlanta. A maze of spatial effects incorporates 30 or so pre-existing artworks to create a gallery of illusions designed to subliminally educate children about the uses of space in the everyday environment. The works shown demonstrate how various artists have depicted space. A model of the sequence of rooms ends the exhibit.

Blue Ridge Chapter. Handley Library alterations and additions, Winchester, Va. (above); Smithey & Boynton, Roanoke, Va., and Russell Bailey & Associates, Orange, Va. The architects were asked to design an addition whose exterior "complements rather than repeats" the style of Barney & Chapman's abundantly ornamented 1908 Beaux-Arts library. The facade restates the old building's voids rather than its forms. Alterations to the old structure, listed on the National Register of Historic Places, include renovation of the basement auditorium, enlargement of its stage and provision of a new lobby, as well as restoration of the copper dome and its stained glass inner dome.

Midway Church of Christ, Tazewell, Va. (below); J. Robert Ferguson, AIA, Abingdon, Va. The focal point of the church is a 45-foot-high tower that can be seen from several miles away in every direction. Its high windows admit changing plays of light into the choir and baptistry below. For its hilltop site, the congregation wanted a strong building free of traditional trappings. Because of the group's modest means, the architect had to economize on materials and use space to maximum advantage. One measure was natural ventilation aided by operable clerestories, accessible from a walkway built into the roof trusses.

Northern Virginia Chapter. Christ the Redeemer Parish Center, Sterling, Va. (above); Lawrence Cook, AIA, & Associates, Falls Church, Va. The architect chose what he calls a "bold, geometric form that says 'church,'" so that the building's purpose is clear to auto passengers on the nearby highway. The three major rooms are arranged axially so that when partitions are removed the space can hold up to 700 people. Clerestory windows admit natural light into this area, and skylights provide light to other interior spaces.

For energy conservation earth berms are placed against exterior walls, and the north wall is buried.

Washington, D.C., Metropolitan Chapter. Frances and Armand Hammer Auditorium, Corcoran Gallery of Art, Washington, D.C. (below); Francis D. Lethbridge & Associates, Washington, D.C. The hemicycle at the north end of the 1897 building was originally a two-story sculpture studio. Early in the 1900s the space was changed into a studio at the upper level and a small auditorium at the lower level.

The auditorium has recently been remodeled as an area for lectures, small seminars and concert or chamber music performances. The floor was rebuilt to provide full, stepped-down, semicircular seating. The stage was redesigned as a focal point of the seating. The cove lighting from the edge of the ceiling was removed, the ceiling was painted dark blue and has multipurpose downlights and stage projectors. A classical triple door motif was introduced on the rear stage wall, and the foyer was remodeled.

Washington, D.C., Metropolitan Chapter.
House addition and remodeling, Washington, D.C. (above); Hartman-Cox, Washington, D.C. The architect's intent was to blend the new with the old, a two-story stone, wood and stucco house. On the first floor the kitchen was extended and a new family room, porch and deck were added. The exterior rim of the family room is enclosed by glass panels, whose outline is repeated on a trellis outside the kitchen. The deck overlooks the new swimming pool. A bedroom and deck were added to the second floor.

Potomac Valley Chapter. R. E. Ward Building II, Rockville, Md. (left); Donald N. Coupard & Associates, Rockville. The client requested a high profile contemporary building that would appeal to "local high-technology corporations." The architect's design response for this 107,000-square-foot speculative office building is a sleek structure of metal wall panels, whose front facade is embellished with semicircular windows framing a long, setback window. The building is fronted with a red metal railing, which marks the transition from the garden area to the building's entrance. A three-story atrium serves as the entry.

Baltimore Chapter. Struever Brothers & Eccles, Inc., offices, Baltimore (above); Cho, Wilks & Burns, Baltimore. A warehouse in the Mount Vernon District was renovated into 2,000-square-foot office space. The new offices were "developed as a sequence of events," in the architect's words, with the "more refined and conservative" renovation on the Charles Street entrance to the "warehouse area" in the rear with exposed structure and ductwork. Light entering through skylights and windows on the north and east facades meet most of the lighting needs.

Beachwood Place, Cleveland (left); RTKL Associates, Baltimore. Since the 225,000-square-foot retail center is located next to a highly affluent residential community, the developer wanted a mall that was "rich and elegant." A sloping site allowed for entrances on two levels. The upper level with its low profile is designed to respond to the adjacent houses. The other facade relates to neighboring midrise apartment buildings and a highway. The sloped standing-seam metal roof screens the mechanical equipment. Inside, a succession of two-story courtyards leads to the two department stores. Each court is designed with a "character" of its own, and has fountains, sculpture benches, tropical plants and antique clocks.

Leonard Evantash

O. Baitz, Inc.

Philadelphia Chapter. Renovation of the Philadelphia Bourse (above); H2L2 Architects/Planners and Evantash Associates, Philadelphia. Constructed in 1893 as the city's commodities exchange, the building suffered neglect from the 1930s to the late '70s. In the renovation the original three-story central space was opened up into a 10-story enclosed atrium. The perimeter walls of the atrium were replaced with a curtain wall system so that the surrounding offices could view the main floor level. A mezzanine was introduced to provide additional commercial space, and parts of the main floor were opened for stairs leading down to restaurants and additional shops in the basement. Wrought-iron and marble stairs were retained from the original building.
Pennsylvania Society of Architects. Fire Station No. 15, Scranton (left); Leung Hemmler Camayd, Scranton. The fire station received a new facade crowned by a parapet that echoes the roof line of surrounding buildings and decorated with a stylized Palladian arch and overscaled emblem. Interior renovation included the addition of a bathroom and mechanical room on the ground level and reversing the location of the lounge and dormitory on the second floor so that the sleeping area is now in the rear. A kitchen is connected to the lounge, and bathroom and locker facilities are adjacent to the sleeping area.

163

Ron Ellis

New Jersey Society. Milford Reservation Solar Conservation Center, Milford, Pa. (above); Kelbaugh & Lee, Princeton. The building, which serves as an educational environmental center for school children and adults, has a dining hall, dormitory facilities for 110 people, two classrooms, a library, lobby and offices. It is designed to be a "model of natural heating and conservation," in the architect's words. Seventy-five percent of the space and water heating needs will be provided by trombe walls, water walls, direct gain and hot water preheating. Night vents and berming are incorporated to eliminate the need for summer airconditioning. The style of the 16,000-square-foot building, which is located on a 1,600-acre site on the northeastern edge of the Pocono Mountains, is meant to evoke images of the farm buildings in the area.

New Jersey Society and New York State Association. Schmidt residence, East Hampton, N.Y. (right); Ronald H. Schmidt, New York City. In this weekend beach house the guest bedroom, study and bath and the carport occupy the first floor; the kitchen, two-story living/dining room and a deck the second, and the master bedroom suite with bathroom, dressing room and deck, the third. The client requested an "optimum view" of Long Island Sound to the east and privacy from the surrounding buildings and a road to the south and west. Therefore, the eastern facade consists mainly of large windows, while openings are minimized on the three other sides.

O. Baitz, Inc.

New York State Association. Usdan Center for the Creative & Performing Arts, Wheatley Heights, N.Y. (above); Johansen & Bhavnani, New York City. Located on 250 acres, the summer center has approximately 50 buildings, most of which are stylized wood sheds. Four new buildings were added: a chorus shed, multipurpose building and twin art buildings (one is shown above). For the design of these buildings the architect chose a "minimalist" design that uses light-weight, industrial materials and finishes to "achieve a perceptual weightlessness, a dematerialization akin to that achieved by classical ballet," in the architect's words. Corrugated glass fiber canopies cover work spaces. In the chorus shed concrete drainage pipes are placed upended as sound diffusing screen walls.

Eastern New York Chapter. Argus Building, Albany (left); Einhorn Yaffee Prescott Krouner, Albany. The project involved the renovation of three adjacent, five-story masonry structures in the city's historic district. To create a central entrance, the middle building was designed as a five-story skylit atrium with the origing 1867 heavy timber and cast-iron structural frame left intact. A glass-enclosed elevator was added. Because the three buildings are not in horizontal alignment, the elevator stops at nine different levels. On the exterior the only major change was the addition of a recessed glass wall adjacent to the atrium. The narrow service alley was transformed into a brick-paved pedestrian walkway.

Norman McGrath

Eastern New York Chapter. Albany County Airport Terminal, Colonie, N.Y. (left); Einhorn Yaffee Prescott Krouner, Albany. One of the central features in this 57,000-square-foot terminal is a 176-foot-long skylit "solar court," which is designed to provide 40 percent of the lighting requirements and 20 percent of the heating needs. (The architect estimates the new terminal will use 75 percent less energy than the existing adjacent terminal that has a similar amount of space and was built in 1960.) The skylight has louvers that are controlled by a minicomputer. It is supported by a masonry wall that is designed to collect and distribute solar heat throughout the building.

Rochester Chapter. Gate's residence, Rochester (below); Macon/Chaintreuil & Associates, Rochester. A two-story carriage house with horse stalls and open storage areas on the ground floor and caretakers quarters on the second was renovated into a residence. The first floor consists of entry, dining room and two-story living room. French doors on either side of the centrally located fireplace lead to the rear yard. On the second floor is a den, which overlooks the living room, bedrooms and baths. The east wing contains a large kitchen with raised hearth fireplace for dining.

Rochester Chapter. St. Joseph's Park, Rochester (left); Handler/Grosso, Rochester. The program called for the demolition of a burned-out church and restoration of its landmark tower. However, the architect proposed saving as much of the church's "context" as possible, and in the process created an urban park. Three facades of the church remain and are structurally tied together with concrete. In the park are elements of the old church: a stair that acts as a stage, three stone pedestals that bear plaques telling the church's history and a fountain built of stones taken from it.

Connecticut Society of Architects. County Federal Savings and Loan Association branch office, Stamford (below); Robert Page & Associates, Guilford. A concrete block gas station was adapted for the bank's branch office, which contains six teller stations, a manager's office, staff room, bathrooms and storage space. A 9x60-foot area was added in the rear. The street facade was extended by four feet, which allowed for the addition of classical columns and decoration. The columns are repeated on a smaller scale to mark the entrance.

Connecticut Society. Falls Mill, Norwich (above); Stephen B. Jacobs & Associates, New York City. Situated on the bank of the Yantic River at the base of Yantic Falls, the mill's major buildings date from 1883 and are now the focus of an historic district. Approximately 120,000 square feet were renovated into 120 rental apartments. In the renovation, the old elements —masonry walls, heavy timber framing, four-inch thick plank floors and the window fenestration—were retained and the new elements were carefully interfaced

with the old. The original dyeworks was redesigned as a recreation and social center, and adjacent buildings became a series of three-level town houses. At the center of the mill, the former power house now serves as a museum and office building.

Submarine Base Training Facility Addition, Groton (below); Hartford Design Group, Hartford. The 12,500-square-foot annex houses a simulated undersea attack center and training classrooms for officers and crew of nuclear-powered Trident sub-

marines. The Navy requested a windowless shed that would adjoin the plain red brick block. Instead, the architect introduced glass blocks coated on the exterior with solar-reflective bronze metallic oxide but clear on the interior to admit daylight. The blocks are intermixed with bricks of the same size. The addition is located on a steep western slope and is structurally independent of the existing building. It is cantilevered over an earth-filled concrete podium, which is anchored into the hillside with rock bolts.

Frederick E. Paton

Connecticut Society and New England Regional Council. Woodbury Place condominiums, Woodbury, Conn. (left); Atelier Associates, Cheshire, Conn. For this small planned community of 24 houses located in an historic district, the local historic commission requested that the design harmonize with the colonial atmosphere of the area. The architect, wishing to avoid "pseudo-colonial" copies, derived most of the residences' details directly from buildings within Woodbury, but also borrowed more stylized details from the New England vernacular. To create a "street feeling" each house has street side mailboxes, front walks and maple trees lining the street.

New England Regional Council. Marketing Corporation of America corporate headquarters, Westport, Conn. (below); Bruce Campbell Graham Associates, Westport. A 1900 warehouse was renovated and an addition made to it. The renovation involved sandblasting the brick walls and exposing the building's heavy wood joists. The ground floor of the warehouse was made into an arcade with a view of the river. The three-story annex is connected to the original warehouse with an atrium that is designed to repeat the arcaded motif of the main building. Red brick, laminated wood beam spandrels and exposed wood decking of the new building complement those of the old.

New England Regional Council. The School House, Boston (right); Graham Gund Associates, Inc., Cambridge, Mass. Ten classrooms on two levels of a former school have been redesigned as one- or two-bedroom apartment units. Living rooms at the corners allow double exposure through the large schoolhouse windows. Former wardrobe, stairway and hall spaces are master bedroom suites. On the ground floor are five more units, three with outdoor terraces. And in the attic area are six units with recessed outdoor decks. The design was the winner of a competition held by the City of Boston.

Acumeter Laboratories, Marlborough, Mass. (below); Architectural Resources Cambridge, Inc., Cambridge, Mass. A manufacturing company of specialized industrial equipment is housed in this 55,000-square-foot building. The use of masonry, sloped roofs and chimney-shaped "monitors" is meant to reflect the architectural characteristics of a New England mill. The building steps back on both sides and is earth-bermed to reduce its bulk and conserve energy. The long monitors on the north and south facades admit natural light into the interior. Down the length of the south facade is a central crane for distribution of raw materials. The middle monitors house the mechanical system. There are skylights on the sloped corrugated steel roof on the north side.

Steve Rosenthal

Steve Rosenthal

170

New England Regional Council. Braintree Station Complex, Braintree, Mass. (above); Parson Brinkerhoff Quade & Douglas, Inc., Boston. The complex, which is now the southern terminus of the Massachusetts Bay Transportation Authority's rapid transit red line, serves trains and buses and has a 1,200-car garage. To blend in with the surrounding residential buildings, the architect designed a low profile structure by locating the station lobby beneath the platform and setting the first floor of the four-level garage eight feet below grade. The garage and station lobby are linked by an aerial walkway and a pedestrian passage through the canopied busway.

Maine Chapter. Samoset Resort Inn, Rockport (left); The Maine Group, Rockport. Located on a 235-acre site on Penobscot Bay, the resort has a 150-room hotel with dining rooms, bars, lounges, meeting rooms, shops and kitchen; a sports center with indoor tennis courts, swimming pool and pro golf shop, and banquet and convention space for up to 600 people. The bedrooms are housed in four-story wings of prestressed lift slab concrete construction. The two-story lodge, reception and dining area is built mainly of heavy timber salvaged from the Grand Trunk grain elevator in Portland, Me. The sports center consists of three interconnecting rigid metal frame buildings.

A5 式
10-15